THE TASTE OF BETTER LIVING - A GUIDEBOOK ON MINDFULNESS

PHALGUNI AGRAWAL

Clever Fox®
PUBLISHING
Chennai • Bangalore

CLEVER FOX PUBLISHING
Chennai, India

Published by CLEVER FOX PUBLISHING 2026

ISBN: 978-93-7500-968-9

CONTENTS

PREFACE

The Journey from Mindful Scrolling to Mindful Living

When I began writing *Mindful Scrolling*, it was not just another project or guidebook — it reflected my own transformation taking shape on paper.

Every thought, every suggestion I offered had been lived, tested, and quietly learned from.

In many ways, I was my own first student, fumbling through lessons of awareness and acceptance. Each time silence won over noise or awareness replaced habit, it became clear that mindfulness was not confined to screens — it was a mirror showing how I was living my entire life. It started in small ways — choosing when to scroll, what to consume, and what to release. Those pauses, as tiny as they seemed, opened something much deeper within me. A quiet voice began to ask: *What if this awareness could stretch beyond the screen? What if mindfulness could find its way into the way I breathe, eat, speak, move, and heal?* That single question became the seed from which *Mindful Living* began to grow.

I never wanted to create another self-help manual or echo the wisdom already beautifully expressed in books like *Ikigai*. What I longed to write was something more personal, more grounded — something that spoke to the quiet corners of everyday life where we often lose ourselves. To me, mindfulness was not a philosophy to study, but an experience to live — something real, raw, and deeply human.

The journey toward that realization, however, was anything but graceful. It was born out of heartbreaks, disappointments, and pain — both visible and invisible.

There was a time when my personal and professional struggles swallowed every ounce of energy, leaving my health quietly unattended. Ganglion cysts appeared on both wrists, a muscle rupture followed, and a constant ache in my shoulder became a daily reminder of limitation.

For someone who lived through words, the irony was painful — my very hands, the tools of creation, were giving up on me.

Some days, holding a pen felt like carrying a mountain; some nights, my mind raced far ahead while my body lagged. Alongside the physical pain came the guilt of feeling like a burden to my loved ones. There were moments of helplessness, frustration, and even quiet anger — especially when it felt unfair. I barely used gadgets, lived with moderation, yet found myself suffering. Others seemed fine without any discipline or exercise, and it was hard not to wonder why my body felt so fragile.

Both heart and body ached in ways words could never fully express. Motivation was fleeting, and energy often felt like a stranger. Even my love life at the time was not blossoming as imagined, though somehow that part felt less heavy compared to what my body was enduring.

Yet, through it all, something within refused to give up. Perhaps willpower has its own kind of stubborn grace.

Despite hating every visit to the physiotherapist, I could not bring myself to rely on medicines alone or surrender to despair. A quiet conviction began to take shape — that healing must come from within. Curiosity soon replaced resistance as I began exploring how yoga, meditation, and mindfulness could repair what pain had broken.

I was not trying to become an athlete; I simply wanted to reclaim the energy of everyday life — to move freely, live independently, and visit my family doctors not for ailments, but for the joy of sharing good news. Three long years of patience, effort, and quiet determination followed. Little by little, my strength returned — not just to my body, but to my spirit.

Somewhere in the middle of that slow healing, mindfulness began to weave itself into every aspect of my life. It was no longer just a practice; it became a way of seeing, a way of being.

And somewhere along that path, when least expected, I met someone who would later become not only my partner in love but also my source of inspiration — someone who reminded me that healing is not just about recovery, but about rediscovering the courage to live with openness again.

A new beginning, a new chapter of my life began with someone — marriage, a new home, and the unique rhythm of army life.

Far from my family, I was surrounded by silence and responsibilities — and that silence became my teacher. I missed my parents, my old life, and the easy familiarity of home. But in that longing, I found something precious: *myself.* I became aware of how I ate — not just what I ate, but how each bite nourished me.

Positivity, an excellent partner, and opportunities were waiting for me. I became aware of how I moved — not chasing perfection, but understanding my body's language. I became aware of how I spoke to myself — no longer with impatience, but with compassion. Every act — cooking, stretching, breathing — became a small ritual of awareness.

I realized the fear of losing a habit was delaying its start.

I made a conscious choice to prioritize today—to savor the liberty of this slow morning *now*, rather than worrying if my future schedule would allow it

This moment is my commitment: to begin the practice of mindful living, knowing that I will inevitably falter and start again.

I promise myself not perfection, but persistent awareness, striving to be present as fully as I can, one moment at a time.

That was when I understood that *mindful living* is not about changing your life overnight. It is about noticing it — moment by moment — until noticing itself becomes a way of being.

Through every conflict and demanding duty, I attempted to strive for greater self-awareness and i continue to do so. It can be overwhelming to manage the rush of household and family responsibilities, especially supporting a dedicated partner alone, without the help of absent loved ones.

Yet, even amidst the constant effort of running a home and caring for someone serving their country, I intentionally 'steal' and cherish those tiny, invaluable moments just for myself." Some readers might find this journey reflective and slow, while others may find within its quiet sparks of recognition — reminders that healing begins not with control, but with awareness.

For me, mindfulness is no longer just a word; it is the way I write, love, move, and breathe. It is what turned my pain into purpose.

And as I looked around, I realized I was not alone in this struggle. I saw so many people — friends, strangers, families — rushing through their days, burdened by noise, expectations, and silent exhaustion. Many of them wanted to live mindfully, to find balance, yet did not know where to begin. Watching this quiet chaos stirred something within me.

I wished I could reach out, hold their hands for a moment, and tell them that healing and awareness are possible — that they already exist within us. That wish, that desire to help even a few souls find their own rhythm of mindfulness, became one of my strongest motivations to write this book. If my words can make you pause for a moment, look inward, and find even a fragment of peace, then I will know that my journey — through all its ache and awakening — has come full circle.

In this book, I have gathered what I observed, learned, and practiced, and what I am still trying to practice in the present tense. These are not grand theories but lived truths — small shifts that anyone, regardless of circumstance, can try. It is about finding calm amid chaos, joy within routine, and meaning in what seems ordinary.

The path will not be perfect; impatience and negativity will surface as they do for me as well, but be committed to learning.

With love, awareness, and gratitude,

Phalguni Agrawal

ACKNOWLEDGEMENT

This book reflects many hearts, hands, and souls who have contributed, knowingly or unknowingly, to my journey. Each of you has shaped a part of who I am — and without your love, patience, and faith, this book would have remained just a dream.

First and foremost, to my *husband Ojas*— my constant source of strength, my calm in the storm, and my greatest supporter.

You have given me the freedom to dream fearlessly and the space to turn those dreams into reality. In moments of doubt, you believed; in times of exhaustion, you comforted; and in every season of life, you stood quietly beside me with love, understanding, and unwavering faith. Thank you for embracing every version of me — the writer, the dreamer, and the fragile human behind it all.

To my *parents*— Kamal Kishore Malpani and Taruna Malpani the roots of my being. You have been my guiding stars, offering not only unconditional love but also the wisdom that anchored me through every storm.

My father's practicality and quiet encouragement, and my mother's endless patience and insight, have been the pillars of my strength— our *Mini sessions* have been my emotional classroom, a space where thoughts turned into clarity and confusion into peace. You taught me to look at life not as a struggle, but as a continuous practice of awareness. I owe much of my mindfulness to your quiet wisdom and your ability to see light even in the darkest corners.

To my *in-laws*, Brigadier Ripu Soodan and Mrs. Shobha Soodan — your guidance, grace, and affection have always inspired me. Thank you for showing me strength wrapped in humility, and for standing with me no matter the distance or the circumstance.

To *Colonel J.K.* — thank you for pushing me gently but firmly toward publishing my words. You saw potential in my scattered thoughts and reminded me that writing is not just passion — it is purpose. Your encouragement transformed hesitation into action and dreams into something tangible.

To my *late Taiji*, your final words urging me to keep writing still echo in my heart. You were one of the first to see something in me that I could not yet see in myself. This book carries a part of your blessing, always.

Thank you for standing by me with faith and affection. You believed in me even during the quiet phases when I doubted my own worth. Your support reminded me that consistency grows not just from discipline, but from love.

To my real brother *Jaideep Malpani* and her adorable partner *Mrs. Anushree Kalani Malpani*, whose incredible drive and tireless effort have built a foundation solid enough for me to finally find my own, less hurried pace. I am eternally grateful that your hard work allows me the privilege of slowing down.

The support you both have provided me makes me overwhelmed, and I believe in magic

To my *friends* and a person with a white heart— the ones who have witnessed both my chaos and calm — thank you for embracing me in every mood and moment. You have held space for me in ways I will never forget.

To all my *mentors, schoolmates, batchmates, colleagues, and peers* — you have all been mirrors reflecting humanity in its truest form. Observing life through your stories and emotions has given me a deeper understanding of the human heart — the very essence of this book.

To the *household helpers* who shared my daily responsibilities and made space for my writing — and to my *army ladies*, who took up my duties and stood by me when my family was far away — thank you for being my extended circle of strength and sisterhood.

To my *extended Malpani family, Bansal Family,* and my *maternal side,* and to my new relations, thank you for your prayers, your warmth, and your belief in me. You have been the foundation beneath every step I've taken. To the *Almighty*, whose invisible hand guided me even when I was too distracted to notice — thank You for every unanswered question that turned into wisdom and for every delay that became a blessing.

And to those who were once part of my life but are no longer here — I hold no resentment, only gratitude. Those mutual endings gave me the *headspace and mental clarity* I needed to move forward. Letting go of what no longer served me became an act of mindfulness. Your absence taught me acceptance, and your silence taught me peace. To all of you — family, friends, teachers, and silent well-wishers — thank you for being the energy, the inspiration, and the quiet force behind this work. Every bit of confidence, effort, and resilience I have poured into this book comes from you.

With endless gratitude and love,

Phalguni Agrawal

WHO SHOULD READ THIS BOOK

This book is not for everyone — and that is intentional. It is not written for those who had their paths carved for them by privilege, nor for those chasing comfort without purpose.

It is for the seekers, the ones who have questions no one around them seems to ask.

This book is for people like you and me — those who've doubted themselves, failed fast, feared deeply, and yet kept walking.

It's for the quiet souls who once tried to please everyone, who held their dreams close but lacked the courage to take that bold leap. It's for anyone who wants to live peacefully — not as a celebrity, but as a whole, fulfilled human being.

It's for the ones tired of external validation, the ones who wish to let happiness spring naturally, without filters or hashtags.

It's for the mothers and fathers balancing responsibilities but yearning for calm, for the young adults who were bullied but never spoke of it, and for those still battling old habits and heavy thoughts. It's for the dreamers who have faced torment and yet are still willing to change.

And yes — if you're a millionaire but humble enough to keep learning, you're welcome here too.

But if you're looking for shortcuts, quick fixes, or magic pills, this book isn't for you. Mindfulness isn't a one-day miracle. It's a practice — one that starts small, grows quietly, and transforms deeply. This book is a truth-teller, not a trend.

WHY YOU SHOULD READ THIS BOOK

There are countless books on *mindfulness* — and yet, most skim the surface. They teach the *how*, but rarely the *why*.

They give you techniques, but not the truth. This book doesn't promise perfection.

It promises a process. Because real mindfulness isn't a soft glow of instant peace — it's messy, challenging, and painfully real.

There will be days when your mind feels empty, your body weak, your thoughts chaotic. You'll feel detached, lost, or too aware. But it's in those moments that you're becoming resilient — your inner foundation strengthening silently.

When you choose to practice mindfulness every day, even for a few minutes, you begin to reclaim control over your thoughts, your reactions, your peace. Your definition of success will evolve.

Your conversations, your emotions, your desires — everything will shift. And yes, there will be failures. But those failures will refine you, not define you. Because mindfulness isn't about erasing thoughts — it's about facing them, reshaping them, and still showing up with calm clarity.

To understand why this matters, reflect on what *Suvir Saran* wrote in *The Indian Express* article, *"There's a strange crisis unfolding. Young minds aren't broken by poverty or war or hunger. They're broken by option paralysis, by endless comparisons, by trend-chasing that never leads to truth. And they are exhausted — lonely, sad, entitled, anxious. Not because they have tried and failed, but because they haven't tried and they know it."*

— Suvir Saran, "Smoke, Mirrors and the Starving Mind," The Indian Express (Delhi Edition), July 6, 2025, p.2.

That exhaustion — that quiet ache inside so many — is exactly what this book seeks to heal gently with love and care

This is not a book of theories. It's an invitation — to rebuild your focus, rewire your patterns, and restore the simplicity of being alive in the moment

It offers gentle, practical steps that help you weave mindful living into the fabric of your everyday life—so it becomes a natural, enduring part of you, not a practice you wander toward and drift away from. It guides you through subtle shifts in awareness, allowing mindfulness to rise like breath—effortless, quiet, and beautifully alive.

With simple practices, reflective prompts, and grounded wisdom, these pages invite you to return to yourself, again and again, until presence feels like home.

Each step reveals the wisdom already living around you—the kind we overlook in the rush and noise of ordinary days. Here you will find small, almost hidden acts of awareness, uncommon yet profoundly simple: the pause between thoughts, the truth in a single breath, the clarity that unfolds when we choose to be fully here instead of moving on autopilot.

These are not clichés or general ideas, but gentle reminders of insights we sense but rarely honor—truths life whispers to us in moments we usually hurry past.

As you move through this journey, you'll learn to breathe with intention, act with clarity, and walk with a soft steadiness that the world cannot easily shake.

THE EVENING THAT MADE ME AWARE

It was an ordinary evening—or so I thought. After finishing my household chores and evening prayers, I lit a small lamp, its flame flickering gently against the walls still dressed in the afterglow of Diwali lights. The soft scent of night queen lingered in the air as I poured myself a cup of tea and unfolded the newspaper I hadn't managed to finish that morning.

The world outside seemed peaceful. Inside, too, everything felt balanced—until I turned to the business section of *The Economic Times*. A bold headline stretched across the page: "AI Duet with ASMR – Cheaper, Easier, Quicker." It was presented like a triumph, celebrating yet another innovation merging technology with human creativity.

The article was neat, confident, and assertive—black font, sharp layout, promising growth and profit. But something small and almost invisible caught my attention.

In the far-left corner, printed in a lighter shade of grey, sat a single paragraph—a quiet critique of this same phenomenon. It questioned the long-term effects of such synthetic comfort, hinting at manipulation, at the slow fading of authenticity. It was subtle—too subtle.

If I hadn't been truly present, I might have missed it altogether. That tiny detail became a mirror for something larger. It wasn't just about font sizes or page design—it was about what the world chooses to highlight, and what it quietly hides. The good news was loud, the concerns whispered. And that imbalance spoke volumes.

In that moment, I realized that awareness isn't about grand enlightenment; it's about paying attention to what most people overlook. It's the space between observation and reaction—the pause that keeps our minds from being swept away by the noise. We live in an age where influence is invisible and constant—woven into headlines, colors, algorithms, and tone. To live mindfully today means not turning away from the world, but learning to *see through* it—to stay conscious even as the world tries to guide our attention elsewhere. That evening, with a newspaper in one hand and tea in the other, I discovered that awareness begins not in silence, but in noticing. And once you start noticing, you can't stop.

As AI learns to imitate life, awareness teaches us how to truly live it.

As AI grows smarter every day, the real challenge is not how fast machines can think, but how deeply we can stay aware.

Artificial lights, artificial intelligence, artificial flowers, artificial plants, artificial humans, artificial gas, artificial gravity cabins, artificial insemination, artificial fibers, artificial grass, artificial turf... artificial aquariums, artificial partners. Artificial images, artificial videos, artificial robots, artificial games, and the list goes on and on. Even at this minute, some scientists might be working on some other artificial product, or some teenager might be inventing a gaming app without code, or some tech giant might be announcing their newest generative AI software or a tech update to optimize the workplace and manufacturing process. Whether it is about experimenting for a better future, or saving the existing present, or creating a new reality for ourselves, or having a human-like conversation, or crossbreeding animals, or using them for experiments, or creating an artificial womb-like atmosphere. I think we have done it all. Some of our inventions have helped tremendously, like biogenetics, genomics, artificial transplants, cancer, and childbearing treatments. Just imagine, and you can do it now, and if you do not want to do it yourself, certainly a software would be present to do it for you. Nano Banana, ChatGPT, Meta AI, and so much more are the best examples for them. Recently, AI has been remarkably successful in detecting diseases on a massive scale. Its integration into healthcare systems around the world is giving amazing results — for instance, an AI-powered app that enables a blind person to perceive their surroundings, or AI software detecting the symptoms of epidemic diseases faster than humans. Wonderful, isn't it? In addition, we have created mind-blowing apps and games to keep us entertained or fill us with knowledge all the time.

I think we, the most intelligent species on earth, have created everything we want as per our desire. We have undoubtedly mastered the art of replicating nature to the finest detail. But while we celebrate these advancements, we must not turn a blind eye to the other side of this technological revolution. Just as the mindless manufacturing of automobiles once fueled pollution before we thought of control measures, the unchecked development and production of AI-driven devices, robots, and gadgets could lead to massive e-waste and energy consumption. Without foresight, we may end up solving one problem while creating another. The same consumerist mindset that drives the overproduction of clothes and cosmetics — carelessly disposed of as if the Earth were asleep — could easily extend to AI hardware, further burdening our already fragile environment.

True progress, therefore, lies not just in innovation but in responsible and sustainable use of technology and living mindfully.

For instance, did you ever think about what becomes of the many robots we are manufacturing at such a large scale? What metals are used in their manufacturing, and so on? Are you aware that the manufacturing process for a robot itself contributes significantly to waste generation through the energy-intensive extraction of rare earth elements and other metals, the creation of chemical effluents, and, most critically, the eventual disposal of complex devices as hard-to-recycle e-waste? Even if it includes composites and recycled plastic, it is never degraded. Or taking years to recycle. It is not just the environmental toll but the ethical corruptibility of AI: the sophisticated cognitive systems designed to enforce "ethical" behavior in autonomous robots (like self-driving cars) can be trivially reprogrammed with a single line of malicious code to turn them aggressive or selfish, posing a fundamental risk to security, safety, and societal trust, alongside broader ethical concerns like job displacement and pervasive surveillance. Another example that crosses my mind is of the Timeshift company. A new cryonics facility developed by the company TimeShift aims to freeze human bodies with the hope that they could one day be revived, allowing people to "pause" their lives and potentially outlive catastrophic events or even an apocalypse. The project presents itself as a futuristic solution for those wishing to experience the world of tomorrow, but it raises significant ethical and legal concerns, since frozen individuals are considered legally dead, and many regions prohibit procedures resembling assisted suicide. Scientists also remain skeptical, noting that current technology cannot safely revive a human body after full cryopreservation, making the concept more speculative than practical for now.

There is *no strong evidence* that the facility is operational or advanced to the stage implied. The technology to reliably freeze a human body and later revive it is still beyond our current verified capabilities. Still, I ask myself if it would have been real news, even if the article is plausible in concept but unverified in its specific claims, then also what would people do? I was wondering because nowadays anybody can do anything. As for me, when I read it, I was like, 'Is that even possible?' and "Why would anyone wish to end this life, whatever the reason? Who can say if the future even exists as imagined? After all, it is only a prediction, and historical data guiding us. Today, decisions are increasingly driven by data — even for those who wish to resist it, the world or algorithm leaves little choice. Yet, imagine if the heroes and leaders of the past had thought the same way — surrendering to circumstance instead of challenging it. Humanity might still be living in chains, not just of others' making but of its own. In many ways, that bondage continues — not to rulers, but to technology and desire. For a large part of society, dependence on digital comfort has become a subtle form of slavery. The recent *Millionaire's Bunker* series on Netflix touches upon a similar obsession: the wealthy striving for security in an uncertain world, moving together like a herd driven by fear rather than hope. Science fiction often makes me ponder such futures — worlds shaped by our own ambitions and anxieties. And while these may seem fictional, the line between science fiction and reality is rapidly blurring. Startups, innovators, and think tanks continue to push boundaries, transforming imagination into invention. This scientific journey has never been easy; humanity has struggled, experimented, and learned to weave technology into everyday life. The countless breakthroughs achieved so far have given rise to an age of extraordinary comfort and capability. It is awe-inspiring that just when it seems we have reached the limits of invention, another discovery emerges — a testament to human will, curiosity, and determination."

But don't you think we are overdoing it?

It feels to me that all of us together have permanently switched to the doing mode instead of the thinking-and-then-doing mode. It's like we've forgotten to pause before we act. Read again. Whether it is scrolling or going on a retreat or vacation, or telling the world about it and then coming back to jobs, or attending a get-together before office, and tirelessly managing and juggling personal and professional lives, and family life. We are just going on and on and on. Whether out of social pressure, guilt, comparison, or your own spirit, there is still no time. But really, is there no time? Or our life is now designed in a manner where we think we do not have time for our own health. I believe we are slowly losing ourselves to the idea of the future while destroying the very present that sustains us. The constant momentum of change and the pressure to adapt have transformed life into something unrecognizable. We keep planning for what's next — and yes, planning is necessary in a world where nothing feels certain anymore: jobs, children, healthcare, even the authenticity of what we consume. But aren't most of us stuck in this endless loop of planning and preparing, unable to live in the moment we have? In chasing a better tomorrow, we are quietly destroying the joys of today. We keep running — from place to place, from idea to idea — thinking movement itself means progress. Yet, somewhere in that motion, we have become part of something larger and far more dangerous: *a culture of overtourism, overconsumption, and overexposure.* **The world no longer asks us to *live;* it asks us to *perform.*** Algorithms have learned our weaknesses better than we know ourselves. They whisper what to desire, what to buy, what to believe, until even our thoughts begin to echo their rhythm. And while we think we are in control, we are only dancing to a tune that numbs our awareness and feeds our distraction. Not just children but even adults have become apart of all this. How many of you must have asked yourself as a young parent, what would become of a child when we ourselves are blinded by technology? Many now believe they can survive alone, cocooned within technology and comfort. But pause for a moment and ask yourself: can your mind truly thrive without connection? Can your body sustain without the rhythm of the natural world? Can your soul, however strong, endure in isolation from everything it was born to be part of? The truth is — neither you, nor I, nor the Earth can afford that illusion any longer. So, take that pause — a real one. Look around you. How many trees can you count where you stand right now? How many birds still share the sky you breathe under? Listen closely — the silence that follows is not peace; it's absence. We are busy altering the very concept of life and death, rewriting lifestyles so obsessively that we have forgotten how to live. We exist now as if the world were a screen to scroll, not a home to nurture. The tragedy is not just that we've disconnected from nature — it's that we've forgotten we *are* nature. The Earth never belonged to us; we belong to it. Yet we act as though that truth is inconvenient, as though it can be replaced by artificial lights and digital comfort. Every invention we've created, every device we hold, is a thread that ties us tighter into this web — beautiful, powerful, but suffocating if we never learn to pause. And if we don't stop soon to remember what it means to simply *be* — to feel the air, to see the green, to listen to the song of life around us — we might wake up one day to a world that no longer remembers us either. We've built civilizations out of chaos and turned imagination into reality. But somewhere along the way, the "our" in humanity quietly fractured into "I." The collective spirit that once bound us — the understanding that we rise and fall together — is fading beneath the glare of individual ambitions.

Look at the world around us — from the protests in Punjab to environmental movements in Nepal, to the rising voices of Gen

Z. These are not isolated events. They are the Earth's reflection back to us — the accumulated result of decades of unconscious living. Just recently, microplastics were found in the excreta of fishing cats. Do you know how dangerous it is? Imagine yourself as the last generation to witness snow or penguins. It is like that. That should have been headline news, but it was not. Media, too, has become entangled in political and corporate machinery. And while organizations are fighting to save wildlife and restore ecosystems, the effort is scattered, insufficient, and unsupported by the majority. Why aren't we innovating for nature? Why are robots built to serve households and industries but not our forests, rivers, or oceans?

Why can't we design machines to clean beaches, plant trees, or restore habitats? Very few organizations explore this direction, even though technology could easily be repurposed for ecological good. The imbalance between innovation for profit and innovation for the planet is glaring. Our choices — our endless cycle of production, consumption, waste, and recycling — have destroyed not only our wealth but our planet and our health. We have mistaken overdevelopment for progress.

Our cities expand endlessly with new roads, factories, and malls, while oceans choke on plastic and skies darken with pollution. Fast fashion alone tells a shocking story: a truckload of clothing is burned or dumped into landfills every second. Only 1% of discarded textiles are ever recycled into new garments. Producing a single ton of fabric consumes energy equivalent to several tons of crude oil. Cosmetics, too, carry an unseen environmental price — from packaging that demands massive energy to microplastics that flow through our waterways. Even recycling, while better than nothing, still consumes immense resources. And yet, we scroll. We watch reels of luxury vacations, private pools, and curated perfection while knowing nothing of the growing landfills outside our cities. *We celebrate sales, but not sustainability.* We are aware of new app updates, but not the state of our oceans. This blindness — whether by choice or exhaustion — is what keeps the cycle alive. While a few are awakening to mindfulness and conscious living, the majority remain wrapped in an illusory comfort built on the suffering of nature. Each day, we walk further away from the harmony we once shared with the Earth. From biohacking to cryopreservation, we chase immortality, forgetting that longevity means nothing if life itself becomes unlivable. The signs are everywhere — polluted lakes filled with refrigerators, coral reefs bleaching at record levels, forests burning, and species disappearing. Are we not ashamed? Have we truly forgotten that we are temporary guests here, not owners? Whenever humans have tried to dominate nature, the Earth has responded — through floods, droughts, diseases, and disasters — reminders that balance cannot be negotiated. And amidst all this, loneliness, depression, addiction, and aggression are rising. Despite countless comforts, there is a deep restlessness in modern life — especially among the young. We've lost patience, replaced stillness with stimulation, and measure our worth in likes and views. Even positivity has turned toxic, masking exhaustion with false smiles. The meaning of success has become uniform — as if everyone must live by the same measure. But success was never meant to be identical. If it were, there would be no difference between humans and robots. This collective obsession with productivity and perfection is breeding vulnerability, anxiety, and emptiness. And yes, our children are growing up in this chaos, learning from what we model rather than what we preach. Our instant gratification is costing us more than money; it's costing us our mental, physical, and planetary health. Social media constantly feeds us images of the "ideal individual," shaping our definitions of beauty, success, and happiness. Because the outside world — once familiar, safe, and comforting — has changed.

But have you ever asked yourself: Is it society alone that shapes this illusion, or are you complicit in accepting it? Are you not, perhaps unknowingly, addicted to the comfort of letting others define your worth? These questions disturb me — and if they disturb you too, maybe it's time to stop running and face them. And if we don't pause, reflect, and act now, it may never return. I did. I sat with my discomfort and had a conversation with myself. From that stillness emerged a simple answer: start with mindfulness. I began with yoga, which led me toward awareness — awareness of body, mind, and the larger connection between sustainability, mindfulness, and nature. And then to other mindful practices. Many entrepreneurs and conscious individuals are realizing the same truth — that living mindfully benefits not just us, but the environment and society at large. Yet, for every mindful person, there are thousands still lost in the noise — too busy, too distracted, or too unaware to notice the imbalance. In the pursuit of fame and money, people have grown aggressive and restless.

On one hand, many people are waking up — becoming more aware of their bodies, minds, and the need to reconnect with nature. They are leaving behind the burnout of corporate cubicles, taking bold risks, and starting businesses that reflect purpose, care, and sustainability. They are learning mindfulness and embracing a lifestyle that honors both personal well-being and the planet's health. On the other hand, the majority continue to move in the opposite direction — mindlessly consuming, destroying ecosystems, and chasing an illusion of perfection in the name of self-care. Expensive treatments, medicines, surgeries, and endless material pursuits have become substitutes for genuine peace.

Still, there is hope. And let us not forget humans are extraordinary beings — resilient, inventive, and endlessly adaptive. We have survived plagues, wars, and apocalyptic shifts. There is a way back — a quieter, humbler way. Mindful living is not a luxury; it's a necessity. It's the act of reclaiming awareness in a world that profits from distraction. The time to reclaim balance — for ourselves, our communities, and the Earth — is not tomorrow. It's now. And now, after everything we've witnessed and felt — the noise, the disconnection, the exhaustion — the question remains: how do we begin again? How do we, as individuals and as a society, restore balance to our minds and to our way of living? The answer lies not in another app, invention, or shortcut, but in something far simpler — a return to mindfulness. I remember feeling out of place when I stopped using my phone in public spaces — at airports, in cafés — but soon realized how liberating it was. I no longer felt the pressure to capture every moment; instead, I began to *live* them. I do miss the old world — where train journeys sparked conversations, where laughter echoed between strangers, where connection felt natural. But I've learned that inner peace is its own world — and that's where mindfulness begins. We need to start living, behaving, and conducting every part of our existence *mindfully* — with awareness, intention, and respect for the world that sustains us. This is not about rejecting progress or technology; it's about realigning how we use them. Every choice we make — how we eat, move, speak, build, rest, or consume — carries the potential to either heal or harm. Living mindfully means choosing the path that heals, both for ourselves and for Mother Nature. Imagine living in harmony with nature, where every decision nourishes rather than depletes. To live mindfully with the Earth is not to give up comfort; it's to redefine what comfort truly means — breathing clean air, drinking pure water, feeling the ground beneath your feet, and having the mental peace that comes from knowing your actions aren't harming the very planet that gives you life. When we slow down, listen, and live consciously, our physical and mental health begin to transform. Our choices — what we eat, how we move, what we consume — become rooted in awareness rather than impulse. So before I share the steps on *how* to live mindfully — physically, emotionally, and spiritually — I invite you to pause here with me. Reflect. Don't rush to the next page.

Your mind, that restless "monkey mind," might already be whispering, *"Just skip ahead, get to the solutions."* You can do that, of course. But if you do, you'll miss the very essence of mindfulness — the slowing down, the patience to sit with an idea, to feel its weight before acting upon it. Take this moment to breathe. Let the words settle. Understand the concepts that follow before you apply them. This book isn't meant to be read in a hurry; it's meant to be *experienced.* I leave that choice with you, dear reader — not to test your discipline, but to remind you of your own power to be present. It is deeply sad, isn't it, that even today, our schools do not teach us how to be *human*? We are taught equations, histories, and corporate strategies — but not how to live mindfully, how to feel deeply, how to manage our emotions, or how to understand the world within us. We learn how to lead teams and manage offices, but not how to manage our own lives. No curriculum teaches emotional intelligence, self-awareness, compassion, or balance — the true foundations of a peaceful existence. So here, in these pages, is an attempt to fill that silence — to offer what our education and institutions have overlooked. This book is a gentle guide to becoming what the world desperately needs today: *a mindful human being.* Someone who lives with awareness, kindness, and connection — not just with others, but with themselves and with the planet that sustains all life. Still, the encouraging part is that change is always possible. Every individual can work to overcome personal dependencies, both visible and hidden, for in the end, every addiction — acknowledged or not — brings its own loss.

Before We Begin: What Mindfulness Does *Not* Mean

Let us begin from Shuniya—from zero, from the quiet and uncomplicated basics—and slowly rise upward from there. You may already feel familiar with what mindfulness is, or at least believe you are.

But before we hit the refresh button, before we update our understanding, let us pause and ask a question we often overlook:

What is *not* mindfulness? We read countless books, articles, and teachings about mindfulness—how to practice it, how to weave it into daily life, how to breathe our way back into the present. Yet rarely do we turn the lens the other way. Rarely do we stop to explore what falls outside of mindfulness, what disguises itself as awareness but is not, what we may have mistaken for presence.

And this exploration—this inquiry into what mindfulness is *not*—is just as essential, just as revealing, as understanding what it truly is.

What is Not Mindfulness?

If you have never truly sat with this question, take a deliberate pause. Let the noise settle. Watch what definition rises in your mind when you ask yourself—not what mindfulness *is*—but what mindfulness *is not*. Allow the first raw, unpolished truth to surface. A deeper meaning might emerge in your mind and heart if you let it.

Notice it. Hold it gently. Perhaps even write it down.

Because from my own experience, I have learned that mindfulness is not a magic pill you can buy, nor a shortcut to success that sweeps away obstacles with a single breath. It will not make flowers bloom in your garden without your effort, nor transform you into a monk overnight. It will not rescue you from your responsibilities, dissolve your desires, or turn your weaknesses into strengths with the ease of flipping a switch.

Mindfulness is not an escape hatch from the world, nor a guarantee of instant peace, wealth, or enlightenment. It is not a tool for burying your emotions, silencing your fears, or pretending everything is fine. It does not ask you to appear spiritual, wise, or eternally serene in front of others. It is not a trend to follow, a performance to maintain, or a hashtag to display. It does not demand perfection. It is not a destination on a map, not a physical place you can travel to, nor some mystical realm where one gets lost and found. And mindfulness certainly does not require that you indulge in self-care rituals 24/7. Attending a weekend workshop, watching a dozen motivational talks, or posting inspirational quotes cannot cultivate true mindfulness if you return to the same unconscious patterns the moment life tests you again. Mindfulness isn't about being calm all the time. It's about noticing when you're *not* calm, and choosing not to spiral. It's about managing your emotions — not deleting them. Maybe you get angry easily. Maybe you stress-shop or overthink. Maybe you constantly replay conversations in your head. Mindfulness helps you pause, step back, and see the pattern before it takes over. It won't make you perfect, but it will make you aware. And awareness changes everything. It's not just mental.

Mindfulness affects your physical world, too. You'll notice how your body feels, how much energy you waste on small worries, and how much lighter life gets when you focus on one thing at a time. And slowly, as you practice, you'll see the ripple effect. When you're calmer, your family feels it. Your pets sense it. Even your surroundings seem softer.

A mindful person changes the atmosphere of a room without saying a word. So why practice mindfulness? Because life isn't waiting. Moments are passing right now — this second. You don't need to be anywhere else or anyone else. You just need to *be here*, fully. Mindfulness doesn't take time; it gives it back to you. Start small. Notice your breath. Feel your footsteps. Taste your food. Listen without planning your reply.

One mindful moment at a time — that's all it takes.
Because in the end, mindfulness isn't about escaping life.
It's about finally arriving in it.

Before you step into that understanding, linger here for another breath. Let the mind soften around what it is *not*. Because only when you clear that space—when the illusions fall away—does the real essence have room to appear.

Mindfulness gently reminds you: peace isn't about doing more, it's about noticing more. **It's not about quitting your job or escaping your reality; it's about being *fully alive* in it.**

A single mindful breath can slow down racing thoughts.
A mindful pause before you reply can prevent regret.
A mindful moment can make an ordinary day feel extraordinary.

Mindfulness gently brings us back to ourselves. It reminds us that peace does not come from doing more, but from being more aware of what we are already doing. It is not about isolating yourself from the world but about participating in it with full attention and sincerity.

What Mindfulness Really Is

When you hear the word *mindfulness*, what is the very first thing that rises in your mind? Don't analyze it, don't filter it—just observe the thought that surfaces on its own. Perhaps you picture someone meditating in stillness, or think of minimalism, slow living, a beautiful dancer lost in art or heightened awareness. Maybe you associate it with being careful, paying attention, or recalling a meaningful workshop you once attended. But when you observe closely, you realize something important: there can never be a single, neatly packaged definition of mindfulness. Its meaning stretches far beyond one idea or practice. It is vast, layered, and deeply personal—shaped by your experiences, inner landscape, and the way you meet life itself. But at its heart, mindfulness means being present and fully aware of the passing moments in life.

It is a beautiful experience of accepting every moment as it is and being aware of that moment. It's about being conscious of your actions and slowly choosing the ones that benefit you, your body, your mind, and the world around you. It's about noticing what's happening around you and within you without rushing to change or judge it.

It's discipline mixed with compassion. It's the art of letting go when needed and moving forward with understanding. It is a way of living where your heart and mind walk together. It's a journey where you are both the traveler and the destination. Mindfulness is not about eliminating discomfort but about being at ease with it.

Jon Kabat-Zinn, in his book "Falling Awake," describes mindfulness as "the awareness that arises when we pay attention, on purpose, in the present moment, and non-judgmentally."

It reminds us that mindfulness isn't about achieving an ideal life but about being fully awake to the one we already have. Similarly, in "A Monk's Journey to the Arctic," mindfulness is seen as the ability to remain present even in harsh or uncertain conditions.

Stillness, the author says, isn't the absence of movement but the presence of awareness. Both ideas point toward one truth—mindfulness is not about withdrawal from the world; it is about engaging with it deeply and consciously.

It's not something you can learn in a week—it's a lifelong process.

Real mindfulness doesn't make noise; it quietly transforms you from within. It's not something to display or talk about all the time; it's something to feel deeply and live consistently.

A mindful life is about making deliberate choices—doing what's right for your health, your growth, and your surroundings. It's about giving your best effort in what you do while staying kind to yourself. It could mean helping a neighbor plant a tree, learning from children without judgment, or sitting quietly in your room without needing a phone or someone's presence to feel complete. Life is not a straight path, and failure is an inevitable part of every journey. Even when we work hard and plan well, things sometimes fall apart. Mindfulness does not erase the pain of failure, but it softens its impact. It helps us face challenges with patience, resilience, and clarity.

When you practice mindfulness, you start to see setbacks not as personal defeats but as moments of learning. You notice your emotions without letting them take over, and slowly, you find the strength to begin again.

That's the quiet power of mindfulness—it doesn't change what happens to you, but it does change how you meet whatever happens. Some of you might feel confident that you already have that kind of control.

But there's no harm in checking in with yourself again, asking a few honest questions, and improving whatever control you think you already have. And that naturally leads to the bigger question—why practice mindfulness at all?

Why exactly should you practice it in daily life? – Separate chapter opening or para

Understanding what mindfulness truly is—and what it is not—was your first step.

The next step is to explore the deeper reason behind it. Why do you want mindfulness in your life? *Understanding the "why" matters because it keeps you consistent even when motivation fades.* And this "why" isn't the same for everyone. It won't be identical for you and your best friend, even if you share the same job, the same home setup, or the same daily routines. It can still vary, and that's completely okay. Knowing your "why" gives meaning to your "how." And when the reason is clear, mindfulness naturally turns from a practice into a way of living. But in general, why is it important for us, the ordinary beautiful people?

We live in an age of overstimulation—notifications, deadlines, endless comparisons, and constant noise. **We are always reacting, rarely reflecting.**

Most of us live in fast-forward. We wake up scrolling, rush through the day, check a dozen apps, jump between messages, and somehow forget to just breathe. Our minds are constantly switched on, trying to be everywhere, and we've forgotten how to simply *be here.*

That's where mindfulness comes in.

Not as another task on your list. Not as a new trend. But as a pause — a moment to return to yourself.

Science supports this ancient wisdom. Research shows that mindfulness practice can lower anxiety and depression, increase attention span, and improve emotional balance. It enhances creativity, strengthens the immune system, and helps us respond more calmly to stress.

Studies on neuroplasticity—our brain's ability to change and rewire itself—show that mindfulness strengthens neural connections related to focus, empathy, and self-control while calming areas of the brain linked to fear and overreaction. In other words, consistent practice can literally reshape your brain for the better. When you cultivate mindfulness, its benefits do not stop with you. Your peace naturally extends to others—your family, friends, pets, and even the environment. The calmer you create a calmer your home.

Mindfulness helps manage emotional impulsivity. It does not make you emotionless, but it gives you space to choose your reaction. I will share my own example with you here. I used to get angry easily.

As a kid, I was quiet in public but easily angered in private—constantly hurt inside, overly sensitive, and selfish without meaning to be. Over time, small moments of practicing mindfulness slowly changed me.

And although I still experience a bit of short-temperedness and other old patterns, I've become so much more aware of my trigger points and of myself.

Mindfulness won't erase your anger overnight, but it *will* soften its intensity and help you respond thoughtfully instead of reacting on impulse. I say this from personal experience.

The shift from being a short-tempered, loud, argumentative child to becoming a calmer and stronger person is something I can see clearly now. For example, earlier, even a small comment—like someone saying the dinner was too salty—would set me off. I'd get emotional, defensive, and irrational, trying to argue my way into control, only to end up drained.

Today, mindfulness helps me notice that first spark of anger, pause, and observe it without judgment. Instead of exploding, I choose a softer, measured response. That simple pause breaks the cycle of overthinking and replaces the exhausting need to be right with the peaceful confidence of just accepting the moment as it is. Similarly, mindfulness can help you with habits like stress-shopping or overindulgence.

It allows you to recognize when you're acting from emotion rather than awareness, helping you slow down and make choices that serve you better. Many people seek external motivation to stay inspired, but mindfulness teaches you to listen to the voice inside.

That voice—soft, honest, and aware—creates lasting change. You do not need to chase constant happiness or avoid sadness; mindfulness helps you live fully in both. It allows you to experience life as it is, with acceptance, curiosity, and courage. In the end, mindfulness isn't a task to complete—it's a way of being that makes your moments richer, your actions more intentional, and your heart more at peace.

Why Practice Mindfulness

You wake up.
You scroll.
You rush.
You reply.
You repeat.
Days blur.
You're everywhere — yet not really here.
That's the modern world.
Fast, loud, endless.

And somewhere in between, you lose touch with the quiet inside you.

Mindfulness is the gentle art of returning to yourself.
It's the pause between chaos and calm.
The breath you take before reacting.
The awareness that says, "Wait. I'm still here."

You don't always need incense, retreats, or silence to be mindful.

You just need to notice — the sip of your morning coffee, the feel of the sun on your skin, the sound of your own breath.

Start small.
Notice one breath.
One sound.
One moment.
That's all it takes.

Finding Your Why…

Before leaping into the ocean of mindfulness, know this: a strong *why* is essential. Your powerful reason will be the engine for motivation and the root of consistent practice. Perhaps your 'why' is shedding a stubborn habit, increasing concentration, or simply feeling more alive and happier without constant gadgets. How do you discover this 'why'? Start with self-observation.

After a difficult conversation or argument, instead of immediately grabbing your phone or bottling your emotions, start noting down (mentally or on paper) what you feel.

In just a few attempts, you might detect a recurring mistake, a habit, or a pattern of behavior. It may feel uncomfortable, even stupid, but jot it down.

The only thing you need is a genuine willingness to change.

This self-identification is the first step toward achieving mindfulness not just as a *practice*, but as a state of being. To integrate this into daily life, you do not need to sacrifice everything; you just need to be a little selfish with your time in the initial stages.

Once it's a routine, the need for sacrifice vanishes, replaced by a profound peace amidst the chaos.

Remember: your willingness must be personal, not driven by a trend. Your 'why' is utterly unique, even if your situation mirrors a friend's. It's foolish to replicate another person's journey entirely.

The willingness will spring automatically when you are truly driven; no one can push you for that.

Mindfulness is an organic process based on instincts and self-observation—it's not an artificial technique. While mentors and experts have tried countless methods to create a path for you, their role is only to guide. In the end, you are the implementer. The journey demands an initial period of detachment and extreme determination, but the reward is a life lived fully awake.

MINDFULNESS: DO YOU REALLY NEED A ZEN GARDEN OR WILL THE BATHROOM DO?

Physical space a barrier or not?

One of the common myths about mindfulness is that it's meant only for a privileged few — for those who can afford retreats, workshops, or beautifully designed homes. That is not true. Mindfulness belongs to everyone. A student living in a shared hostel can live mindfully. A parent managing a small apartment can practice mindfulness daily. A person with limited income can bring awareness into the smallest moments of life — while cooking, cleaning, or walking to work. What truly matters is not your physical setting, but your intention and consistency. Your determination defines your practice.

Your priorities shape your path. The "barrier" of space exists more in the mind than in your surroundings. If you believe you can't practice mindfulness because of where you live, start by working on that belief first — because mindfulness begins right there, in how you perceive your own limits.

To practice mindfulness, you do not need a perfect setup or a special room filled with soft music and scented candles. You do not need mountain air, a silent retreat, or a sea view.

Those things can help, yes, but they are not essential. Mindfulness is not about *where* you are — it is about *how* you are. If you live among people who support and encourage such practices, who give you physical and mental space to grow, that is wonderful — consider it a blessing. But life will not always offer ideal conditions. It's often messy, noisy, and unpredictable. And yet, mindfulness can thrive there too. It's not impossible; it is simply real.

In many Indian households, finding private space can be challenging for both men and women.

Unlike in some Western cultures, living alone isn't always an option or even a preference. But that doesn't make mindfulness unreachable — it simply means your approach will be more creative and flexible.

A personal corner or quiet room can help, yes, but it isn't mandatory. If possible, create a small calming space of your own.

It doesn't have to be fancy or picture-perfect. It could be a cozy corner of your bedroom, a spot on your balcony, a chair near a window, or even a quiet moment on your bed before everyone wakes up. Let it be your pause zone — a place to breathe, read, write, meditate, or simply sit in silence. Keep it simple and uncluttered.

Avoid turning it into a showroom filled with décor or gadgets.

Let it be genuine, calm, and personal. Sometimes, people spend money building extravagant spaces — indoor pools, bars, or entertainment corners — influenced by what they see online.

But true peace doesn't come from *more* things; it comes from *fewer* distractions. You don't need luxury to feel grounded. What you truly need is a space, however small, that allows you to feel free. Think of a small sapling growing between cracks in a rock. It doesn't wait for perfect soil or ideal weather. It simply grows — quietly, persistently. That's mindfulness. Like that sapling, you too can grow in imperfect conditions if you just give yourself a little space — physically, mentally, or emotionally. Even a few minutes of solitude can help you recharge, heal, and return stronger. Sometimes, nothing is wrong with you — you just need space. Not because you dislike people, but because you need to reconnect with yourself. This can be difficult, especially in joint families or busy homes, but it's necessary.

Taking space doesn't mean abandoning your responsibilities or isolating yourself. It means being honest about your need for stillness. Some people around you may not understand it at first. They might mistake your silence for distance. But when you communicate with respect and sincerity, they usually accept it. A short mindful pause — a few hours without your phone, without conversation, simply resting in awareness — can do more for your peace than an entire week of distracted activity.

You don't need luxury to live mindfully. You just need *presence.*

A quiet corner.
A little time.
A calm breath.

That's enough to begin. From that small space, everything else will slowly start to open up.

Now lets us see how you exactly develop a mindset and make mindful living part of your daily life.

DEVELOPING THE MINDSET FOR MINDFUL LIVING

Flexibility plays an enormous role in life, in every aspect. Similarly, establishing a solid mindset and attitude is as crucial as having a strong *reason* to practice mindful living *permanently*. This preparation must precede the actual practice. Without this foundation, you'll find yourself abandoning the practice every few months, drifting endlessly from one workshop to the next. You need a deeper understanding—a true conceptual grasp—of mindfulness before you jump in. We all yearn to make mindfulness a constant, daily state, regardless of our work or environment.

Yet we fail many time, and the majority of us give up because let's face the facts: even the Buddha sought out detachment and a particular environment for enlightenment. But he did not achieve the state he was in a single day. In fact, if you read the story, it was found that he deprived himself of basic things like food, water, sleep, and so on. He almost lived like a beggar, but he felt weak instead of strong and soon realized that he could practice mindfulness without depriving himself of the essentials of life. All of this took years for him. It takes immense effort to calm the internal and external noise, and a quiet space certainly speeds up the process. Yet, life rarely affords us that pristine silence. The real key is mastering the "how" *amidst* the chaos. The true breakthrough, as Buddhist monks have discovered, is that perfect external conditions are not necessary for the mind of non-attachment (*cittaviveka*) to arise. One senior monk, Luang Por Sumedho, even had a profound vision: sitting in a "white, freezing void"—a harsh, featureless wilderness—yet feeling "complete and utter peace". His pilgrimage into the Arctic wilderness was a physical journey to experience this absolute silence, proving that the state of mindfulness can, and *must*, exist even in the most challenging environments.

The Three Pillars of Practice to Develop a Right Mindset for Mindfulness

1. Embrace Your Unique Journey.

You must grant yourself the grace of acceptance. Your mindful journey is uniquely yours, which means your starting point will also be unique. Perhaps, initially, you need a hard push: a combination of yoga, therapy, and a detox program. For your best friend, however, a simpler commitment to just yoga and meditation might provide the perfect head start. Embrace the method that works for *you* and accept that your required 'starter pack' may be entirely different from the next person's.

Similarly, when attending a seven-day yoga program with 700 strangers, your experience will inevitably differ from doing the same practice alone or with a familiar face. You must accept this difference immediately. The greater truth is that you can attain the same depth of satisfaction and the same level of excitement in both situations. It is a long journey to internalize this, but you must be willing to value the total output of your practice—the internal shift—over the external variables like the place, the people, and the temporary excitement.

The most vital act of acceptance is releasing the self-inflicted pressure to achieve mindful living in a few short days, especially at the expense of family or work time. Slow, consistent micro-steps are the secret to longevity. Real consistency requires deliberate space: putting your phone away and dedicating a straight 40 minutes to spiritual and mindful practices. Understand that habit formation takes time—plan for six months to a year. Think of it like a child's education: you don't expect a five-year-old to be financially independent, but you invest years into their schooling for future returns. Mindful living requires the same patient investment.

2. Get Comfortable Saying 'No.'

Secondly, get comfortable saying 'No'. In our constantly demanding world, learning to say 'no' is not just about being polite; it's a powerful act of mindfulness and self-preservation. When we mindlessly agree to everything, we slowly drain our most vital resources—our enthusiasm and our energy. Mindfulness teaches us to pause and check in: Do I genuinely have the capacity, or am I reacting out of obligation? Embracing a respectful 'no' isn't anti-social; it's *pro-well-being*. It's a way of setting boundaries that prevents burnout and allows us to say a true, energetic 'yes' to what matters most. Remember, you don't need to refuse every request, but when you feel yourself stretching thin, a kind and clear 'no' is absolutely required to protect your peace and ensure you show up fully for the commitments you *do* keep. Be bold and resolute when declining over-indulgence or excessive socialization. Don't second-guess leaving a small gathering or avoiding a gossip session. When you prioritize your peace, you are doing the right thing; stop feeling guilty or under-confident about it. It might take months to master this, but it will be worth the solitude.

3. Cultivate the Willingness to Change

Growth is impossible without the willingness to change, and this process is a lot like dating. Being mindful means observing our habits, beliefs, and routines, recognizing which ones are serving us and which are simply holding us back. Instead of immediately committing to a grueling new routine, treat new habits like first dates: explore them, see if you have chemistry, and keep the relationship low-pressure at first. Change can feel daunting, but clinging stubbornly to the familiar because it's comfortable will only stifle your potential. By cultivating an openness to these new, positive actions—getting to know them over time, not forcing an immediate connection—you can eventually marry the truly good ones forever, ensuring your energy and motivation remain fresh, dynamic, and passionately engaged with the future. So, you must have a willingness to change. If you still believe mindfulness is only possible in isolation, you're viewing it as a short-term escape. True mindful living is about aligning *every* daily task with your purpose and doing *everything* with a full heart. The ultimate point of practice is to find peace with yourself and the world you live in—not to leave it permanently. You learn to swim *in* the ocean, not just on the shore.

THE CORE IDEAS BEHIND MINDFUL LIVING-

We are not tired because we do too much—we are tired because we try to do it all perfectly.

Utopian World of Balance.

Let us begin with the word *balance.* A word so small, yet carrying the weight of an entire generation's struggle. We live in an age where everyone is desperately trying to hold things together—balancing a child's birthday celebration right after a yoga session, attending a grand store opening after morning tea, managing our homes, parenting, hosting parties, coordinating household help, setting up selfie stations, and of course, trying to look perfect in every photograph. To me Modern life often feels like one long project management assignment—every hour scheduled, every action optimized, every moment measured against someone else's achievements. We tell ourselves, *"If they can handle it, why can't I?"* and so we push harder, doing whatever it takes to maintain the illusion of balance. But by the time the sun sets, many of us are running on empty—mentally numb, emotionally drained, and quietly unfulfilled. For some, that exhaustion begins even before the day does. We wake up tired, step into comparison, scroll through other people's lives, communicate endlessly.

Amidst all this, we consume an endless stream of advice—countless videos, reels, and motivational talks—all promising the key to achieving harmony between professional duties and personal life. Yet, for some reason, we continually find ourselves tilting off center. Why? Even those who insist they've "found balance" still whisper about needing more "me time," caught in the same cycle of doing everything, everywhere, all at once.

Exactly why? Because in pursuing the relentless cycle and maintaining the so-called balanced life, we lose sight of the simplest truth: balance isn't another task to manage—it's a relationship we cultivate with our own well-being. We have been relentlessly pursuing someone else's recipe for well-being instead of taking the time to design our very own. The definition that defines and matches our own value system, situations, and other uncontrollable factors. We've mistaken imitation for inspiration.

Rediscovering the Self: Foundations of Personal Balance"

We rush from one milestone to the next, often forgetting that life is meant to be lived, not just documented and managed. Perhaps the fault lies not in the striving, but in the definition we are pursuing. Think about any lecture you've heard from a leader, mentor, or guru. Did they ever discourage you from following their principles while encouraging you to craft your own unique path? Probably not. Most of them simply show you the right direction and remind you of the important things to keep in mind—but they don't hold your hand and push you down that path. Their role is to guide, not to control. They offer wisdom based on their experiences, but they also understand that your life, your challenges, and your strengths are different from theirs. What works for them may inspire you, but it doesn't have to define you. So take the teachings, absorb the wisdom, and then implement them in a way that aligns with your journey. Let their words light the way, but let your own steps create the path. Take a moment to truly reflect. Ask yourself—who is setting the standard for balance? Who decided that being in balance means doing it all with a smile? What does a well-ordered life look like *for me*? A definition exclusively according to your standards, likes, and needs? Is there any connection between my liking and needs? What are the crucial components of maintaining this equilibrium? What do experts in human behavior say about this state of affairs? Can a person's existence remain steady regardless of external pressures? Is it realistic to expect every day to be flawless? Have I ever considered why the photographs of my life's moments feel more exciting than the moments themselves? Did I truly capture that experience in your mind and spirit, and not just in an image?

In the world of science, Scientists and researchers have certainly tried to quantify life balance, employing psychometric scales to assess things like Work-Life Conflict (WLC) and overall satisfaction with life (like the SWLS). However, these tools only capture your self-reported perception at a given moment—they don't measure objective reality. The core truth is that because our definition of balance shifts constantly—depending on our age, goals, and daily demands—a simple number cannot capture the full human experience. While the scientific scales offer data points, the real measure of your life's harmony is deeply personal: it's your inner feeling of peace, resilience, and genuine engagement, not a static score calculated on a chart. But the majority of us have not even defined the meaning of our own balance. We are living through an epidemic of *overwhelm.*

Obsession, Perfection, And Misconception

Our obsession with perfect balance has made many of us silently miserable. Quitting feels easier not because we lack discipline, but because we are emotionally overexposed—to deadlines, screens, noise, and invisible expectations. We measure success in hours rather than meaning. We confuse productivity with purpose. For Instance when a child enters your life, chaos becomes natural. You will miss events, skip routines, and lose rhythm. But chaos doesn't mean failure; it means transformation. Your only true responsibility is to nurture your *basic needs* and the *fitness of body and mind.* You don't need to mimic an influencer's perfectly curated life while navigating your sacred, messy, human one. Balance is not for display—it's for living. Balance doesn't mean equal—it means aware. It means understanding that some days you will excel at work but fail at patience, while other days you'll fail deadlines but win love. Perfection isn't the goal; *presence* is. To err is human, and in chaos lies balance; in imperfection lies beauty. But in our pursuit of constant equilibrium, we've forgotten the poetry of fluctuation. No tree blooms all year round, except for the few that are artificially forced to. No human smiles through heartbreak. Yet we expect ourselves to remain in perpetual bloom, and when we fail, we call ourselves inadequate.

Practical, Real-World Examples

For some, true balance simply means tending to their family and their own health. Vacations, parties, and milestones are beautiful, but they are not the foundation—they are bonuses. Even in spirituality, every divine being found peace amidst turbulence. From Kali Ma's cosmic dance to Shiva's meditative stillness, from Jesus's trials to Buddha's renunciation—every path to serenity was forged through struggle. Rama lost his kingdom, his wife, and his brother, yet stood firm in dharma. Nelson Mandela spent 27 years in prison and emerged radiant with forgiveness. Even modern icons like Elon Musk admit to sleepless nights. John D. Rockefeller, the perfectionist behind Standard Oil, micromanaged every detail until stress stole his hair and peace. Meanwhile, Andrew Carnegie delegated, trusted, and strategized—achieving similar success without self-destruction. Two men, one empire-sized dream, and two entirely different fates. The lesson is timeless: control is an illusion, and over-control is a form of self-harm. When you drown in perfection, you lose the rhythm of life. Burnout isn't strength—it's an imbalance wearing a brave face. Look at nature. She teaches balance better than any life coach ever could. She shifts through seasons—spring's bloom, summer's blaze, autumn's surrender, winter's stillness—each essential, none permanent. Yet we demand spring forever. We resist change, forgetting that imbalance and imperfection are not our enemies—they are our teachers. Too much balance can be suffocating, just as too much chaos can be draining. Observe water: it flows around obstacles, never forcing, never competing. Observe a flower: it never compares its bloom to another. If you get injured during exercise, you don't abandon movement—you pause, heal, and return. Likewise, if life throws an imbalance your way, you rest, breathe, and realign.

Happiness all the time is not the goal—authentic living is. Even nature regenerates, sheds, and renews. Why shouldn't you? Remember the tree we drew as children—the one with roots hidden underground? That's you. Growth isn't always visible, but it's always happening. The roots of your peace deepen quietly in moments when nothing seems perfect. And so, life will always come with pending deadlines, unfinished chores, and critical relatives. But amidst this noise, your health and peace must remain your non-negotiables. *Mindful living* doesn't mean escaping life—it means returning to it. It is not another task on your list; it is the pause between breaths that keeps you alive. Because the real question was never *how to balance it all.* The real question is: *how can I live fully, even when things aren't perfectly balanced?*

Perhaps that is where the true *Utopian World of Balance* begins—not in symmetry, not in control, but in graceful surrender to life's ebb and flow. When we stop chasing perfection and start honoring the exquisite mess of being human, we finally find what we were looking for all along: peace, not balance.

Temporary Joy of Materialism

We buy faster than we breathe, yet we still feel empty.

Roti. Kapda. Makaan.

Whether you are a fan of Bollywood or not, you must have heard this famous phrase. It carries far more depth than we realize. If you narrow down all human needs, they fit within these three simple words: food, clothing, and shelter. For centuries, they were enough. They sustained life, dignity, and survival. But somewhere along the way, as our access to comfort grew, our sense of contentment shrank. Exposure to materialism and overindulgence in luxury blurred the once-clear line between *need* and *desire.* The result? A world drowning in consumerism, where the race to acquire has replaced the art of appreciating.

Of course, money and material possessions matter. They provide stability and safety—essentials for any functioning life. But beyond that, it becomes a choice—a test of wisdom. The problem begins when possessions start possessing us. Without realizing it, we have begun to judge people not by their hearts, but by their handbags; not by their character, but by their cars. You may not say it aloud, but silently, in the corners of your mind, you measure others by their income, appearance, and social media aesthetics. And that's where the shift began—from *being* to *appearing.*

The Rise of Needless Desire

Roti, kapda, makaan—our core needs remain unchanged even today. Yet the world around us screams otherwise. Social media, advertisements, and influencer culture have collectively rewritten the definition of "necessity." Endless clothes, endless food deliveries, endless houses filled with things we rarely use—these have become our new "basics."

We are told that we deserve *more.* More comfort, more gadgets, more outfits, more experiences—until the very idea of "enough" disappears. The media's power is subtle yet immense; it doesn't just sell products, it sells emotions—status, validation, belonging.

Today, you can even buy the *pre-loved* outfit of a celebrity, a slice of someone else's spotlight. We have collectively become enchanted by the most trivial things—so much that we are dressing for Instagram more than for ourselves. Whether it's a concert, a café brunch, or a first date, our choices revolve around *how it will look online.* And with endless options comes what psychologists call "option paralysis."

According to *Keep It Usable's* research on the psychology of choice, the human brain performs best with limited options. Too many choices trigger stress, doubt, and regret—a mental overload that leads to dissatisfaction, no matter what we pick. This constant decision fatigue drains our time, energy, and emotional health. We scroll for hours comparing, choosing, abandoning, and restarting—trapped in a loop of digital desire.

Collecting Things, Losing Moments

The temporary joy of materialism is one of the biggest hindrances to mindful living. We have become travelers collecting things—souvenirs, selfies, postcards—instead of memories. We live more vividly in pictures than in presence. Even influencers, who project the epitome of luxury, often crave to disconnect from it all. Yet they can't, because their image is their income.

Our obsession with wealth projection has turned homes into museums and cafés, curated for aesthetic appeal rather than comfort. We collect endlessly—clothes, décor, gadgets—even though half of it gathers dust. Ask yourself, when was the last time you printed a photo of yourself that wasn't perfectly posed or filtered? The candid, awkward, real moments are missing, replaced by digital perfection.

The projection of an affluent life has manipulated collective perception. What we see online isn't always real—it's often rehearsed, filtered, and edited. Ironically, we've made our homes so comfortable that they now resemble cafés, yet we still crave going out. We've designed every corner to look beautiful for others' eyes, but forgotten to feel peace in it ourselves.

When Less Becomes More

Take, for instance, the common modern setup—double income, no kids. On paper, it sounds liberating. But even there, happiness slips away when lifestyle expectations rise. The truth is, even with a modest income and simpler choices, one can still lead a deeply fulfilling life. You might not travel the world or wear couture every weekend, but you'll have the quiet joy of being content.

Mindful consumption doesn't mean renouncing material comfort—it means respecting it. It's about knowing *when enough is enough.* Today, we are buying cheap dopamine in the name of YOLO (You Only Live Once). But what if the real meaning of YOLO isn't indulgence, but *awareness*—a reminder to live wisely, not wastefully?

Buying a new outfit occasionally is fine, but mindless consumption steals more than money—it steals peace. Every unnecessary item takes up space in your home and your head. The new aesthetic trend that blends vintage with modern preservation is a beautiful direction—it honors the past. Yet, our overall habits remain unsustainable. We still hoard counterfeit cosmetics, fast fashion, and gadgets that expire emotionally before they do physically.

Have you noticed how the internet is flooded with videos like *"10 Wardrobe Must-Haves"* or *"How to Style, Not Just Wear"*? The message seems empowering, but subconsciously it breeds dissatisfaction—reminding you of what you lack rather than what you have. So ask yourself honestly: *Are you a mindful shopper?* You might secretly agree that you are not—because like many of us, you've been seduced by the glitter of temporary joy.

The Quiet Shift Back to Meaning

But here lies the hope—awareness. Once you see through the illusion, you begin to crave simplicity again. You begin to value what cannot be bought: peace, laughter, rest, and real conversations. The less cluttered your surroundings, the quieter your mind.

Minimalism is not the opposite of abundance—it's the wisdom to recognize which abundance truly matters. The joy of owning less is that you finally have space—for yourself, for experiences, for silence. You stop living life for the next unboxing and start living it for the next sunrise.

Because in the end, roti, kapda, makaan were never just about survival—they were metaphors for contentment. Food to nourish, clothing to express, shelter to rest. Everything else is extra. And the irony of modern life is that the more we add, the less we feel full.

The *Temporary Joy of Materialism* will always shimmer, but like glitter, it fades quickly—leaving behind the longing for something deeper. And that "something" is what mindful living quietly offers: a return to simplicity, gratitude, and meaning.

Biophilia: The Science of Our Natural Affinity

Have you ever noticed how your mind quiets the instant your bare feet touch beach sand in a warm sun. or your desire to go in the water the moment you hit the beach? The gentle rhythm of waves, the salt-kissed breeze, and the laughter of a child beside you—suddenly, all the clutter of modern life dissolves. That fleeting serenity is not a coincidence; it is the whisper of biophilia—our innate tendency to seek connection with nature and other forms of life. Biophilia is essentially our love of life and all living things, a deep connection hardwired into our DNA. It is the reason we feel an immediate sense of peace when listening to birdsong, or why a simple bouquet can instantly lift our mood in a stuffy room. When we design spaces with natural light and materials—like wood or stone—we are instinctively responding to this evolutionary need for connection.

Origin of Biophila

The word *biophilia* was first introduced by psychologist Erich Fromm (1964) as a "psychological orientation of being attracted to all that is alive and vital." Later, Edward O. Wilson (1984) expanded it into the *biophilia hypothesis*, suggesting that humans possess an evolutionary affinity for natural settings, rooted in millennia of survival among trees, rivers, and skies. In simple terms, nature feels like home because, in our biological memory, it *is* home.

Modern research confirms this truth. Karun et al. (2025) describe biophilia as an affection toward animals, plants, and living systems that has evolved through genetics, shaping human adaptability and creativity. Across cultures and ages, people respond similarly to green landscapes and flowing water—an echo of the ancient savanna biome that once nurtured our species. That's why natural scenes calm the heart faster than city noise and why gazing at trees outside a hospital window can speed healing.

Nature as Healer and Teacher

The Attention Restoration Theory (ART) proposed by Kaplan & Kaplan (1989) explains that time spent in nature restores the mind's ability to focus. Our attention system has two modes—directed and effortless. In cities, we live in directed attention, constantly focusing, deciding, scrolling, responding—until our brains fatigue. In nature, attention becomes effortless; we are drawn, not forced, to notice the rustle of leaves or a bird's call. This "soft fascination" gives the overworked brain a chance to rest and repair.

The biophilic quality of the environment, together with our sense of connection to it, determines how restorative the experience feels. That is why a ten-minute walk under trees can soothe anxiety better than an hour on social media. As Karun et al. (2025) note, *biophilic and restorative theories strongly support the role of nature-based interventions in human health, healing, and resilience.*

Consider the rise of green care farms in Scandinavia, where individuals recovering from depression or chronic illness spend time tending plants and animals. Studies show that such nature-based therapies reduce stress, elevate mood, and improve cognitive performance. Even simple horticultural activities among older adults have been proven to lessen loneliness and enhance vitality.

Biophilia in the Digital Age

Yet, in our urbanized, screen-lit world, genuine nature encounters are fading. Ironically, technology is now attempting to recreate them. Research by Marocco et al. (2025) at the Sapienza University of Rome explored how Virtual-Reality-based mindfulness in simulated natural environments can evoke similar emotional benefits. Participants immersed in virtual forests or beaches showed significant reductions in negative emotions, compared to traditional mindfulness sessions. VR, they suggest, can act as a bridge for those who lack access to real green spaces, helping practitioners regulate emotions and sustain present-moment awareness.

However, as the researchers caution, no digital replication can fully substitute the multisensory dialogue of authentic nature—the feel of soil, the scent after rain, the heartbeat that syncs with ocean waves. Virtual nature can *guide* us back to our roots, but mindful living begins when we step outside and truly listen.

Biophilia and Mindful Living

To live mindfully is, in essence, to live *biophilically*. It means noticing the pulse of life within and around us—the flutter of a leaf, the rhythm of breath, the warmth of sunlight on our skin. Mindfulness invites us to *re-member* (literally, bring back together) the parts of ourselves that have drifted away from nature's rhythm.

When you pause amid daily chaos to look at the sky, you're practicing micro-moments of biophilia. When you choose to walk instead of drive, plant herbs in your kitchen, or meditate near a window, you are honoring the ancient bond that sustains both planet and psyche.

In the words of Barbiero & Berto (2021), biophilia is not merely an aesthetic preference—it is an *evolutionary adaptation* that keeps us mentally and physically balanced. Ignoring it, as modern life often forces us to do, creates the silent epidemic of disconnection, anxiety, and burnout. Mindful living, therefore, is not about escaping the world but about *returning to its natural pulse.*

Biophilia reminds us that healing is not found in constant consumption but in conscious connection. The sea, the soil, and the sky are not luxuries—they are our first teachers of presence. Every moment spent in nature, real or recreated, rewires us toward calmness, empathy, and clarity. As the breeze brushes your cheek or you watch a leaf dance in sunlight, realize this: you are not outside nature—you are nature remembering itself.

The Algorithm Inside Your Head: Social Media and Neuroplasticity

Consider the last time your hand reached for your device before your conscious mind even registered the intent. Can you genuinely recall a single day when you unplugged simply because you chose to—not because a retreat demanded it or a deadline forced it? It is likely a struggle to remember. You might rationalize the habit by claiming the office is always calling, yet that logic often crumbles on a Sunday. Even on this universal day of rest, do you not find yourself subconsciously glued to the screen, scrolling through a feed that never ends? There is a reason for that.

Our brain has started feeling purposeful with our phone in hand. When we do *not* use a social-media platform for a while, there's a subtle anxiousness around us. On one level, we may be thriving — doing well in life, in work, in relationships — yet the *portrayal* of our life doesn't seem enough. It must look perfect, seamless. Enter: the scroll.

Enter: the notification ping. Enter: the dopamine hit.

I know what you're thinking. You've likely read a dozen articles about the 'social media dopamine trap' and are tempted to flip past this section. Please, don't. I'm not here to lecture you on screen time or seek your attention for the sake of an algorithm. I am here because I want you to regain permanent control. We are moving beyond the repetitive 'doom-scrolling' headlines to simplify the actual science of what is happening inside your head.

Even if you think you know how dopamine works, I ask you to register it one more time through this new lens. Why? Because understanding this mechanism is the key to neuroplasticity. We aren't just going to discuss how your brain gets hooked; we are going to learn how to hack that very same system to automate positivity and rewire your life. But for that, you will have to read this section and the steps I have shared at the end of the book. While I'm not going to tell you outright to stop using social media, I do want you to understand what it is doing — how it's rewiring your brain — so that you can choose *mindfully*. Because for permanent change, you don't just attend a mindfulness workshop and hope things improve. You learn how your brain works, you learn emotional-intelligence, you learn habits.

"Your Brain Is Not a Fixed Machine — You Are Shaping It"

Here's one science-fact: the brain wiring is *not fixed*. In fact, your brain is constantly adapting. Imagine your brain as a roadmap; neuroplasticity is the process by which your brain builds new highways for frequent behaviors and lets unused dirt roads fade away. It's making new pathways, weakening others. Digital interactions — especially prolonged ones — leave a mark. Research shows that intense social media or internet usage correlates with structural changes in brain regions tied to reward, attention, and social processing. (PMC)

The brain's Default Mode Network (DMN) is always active — even when we rest. It handles self-referential thought, memory, and future planning.

When you then feed it social media, notifications, endless images, and comparisons, you are layering *additional stimulation* on top of that resting stream.

The result: your brain shifts into a "constant expectation" mode — expecting reward, expecting feedback — and therefore, your capacity for calm, uninterrupted presence shrinks.

What Social Media Does to Your Brain Wiring

Let's break down some of the key ways social media interacts with brain wiring — with effects you might not always notice, but you experience.

1. Attention & Cognitive Load

Social media divides our attention. Rather than focus on one task, we flick between posts, notifications, and replies. This constant switching erodes our ability to sustain focus. A meta-analysis found that engaging in multi-tasking via digital media was associated with significantly poorer overall cognitive performance.

Over time, this means the very brain circuits that support *deep work*, sustained attention, and reflection become underused — or altered.

2. Reward Circuits & Social Feedback

Social media platforms are built around reward systems — likes, comments, shares. According to the Active Inference Framework, we are predictive agents: we anticipate rewards, we adapt based on the gap between what we predict and what arrives. Social media constantly warps this predictive model, making our brains expect *immediate*, *variable*, unpredictable feedback.

In adolescents, habitual checking of social media has been associated with changes in brain regions tied to social reward anticipation (amygdala, ventral striatum, dorsolateral prefrontal cortex).

Thus, your brain becomes wired to crave the next notification, the next image, the next affirmation.

3. Structure & Development

For younger brains especially, social media use correlates with differences in brain structural development — such as cortical thickness or surface area in regions associated with cognition and social processing. Some studies show heavy users have higher baseline thickness in certain areas, but then stronger decreases over time.

While the effect sizes are still small and the evidence evolving, the message is clear: your brain wiring is responsive to how you spend your digital hours.

Why This Matters for Mindful Living

You might ask: *So what?* If my phone and social media are part of life anyway, how does this link to mindful living? Here's the connection:

Mindful living isn't just about doing a breathing exercise or sitting quietly for ten minutes. It is about choice — how you respond, how you steer your attention, how you spend your time—and thus how you *wire* your brain.

When your attention is fragmented, your reward system is hijacked by feedback loops, your brain rewires to expect constant stimulation—you are not fully present. You are not fully *alive.*

By understanding the brain wiring dynamics, you gain power. You can decide: "Today I will check social media only once every hour." Or "Tonight I'll have one hour of screen-free time." Or "When I engage, I will post mindfully, not habitually." Each of these choices rewires your brain toward agency rather than autopilot.

Your brain is not a static machine—it's exquisitely malleable. Social media is changing how we think, how we pay attention, and how we seek reward. If we let it run unchecked, our wiring shifts toward fragmentation, hyper-expectation, and surface-living. But if we become aware—if we apply mindfulness not only to our breath, but to our screens—we can reclaim our attention, and we can sculpt our wiring with purpose.

Think of your brain like clay. Every scroll, every ping, every click leaves an imprint. Today, you might not feel the difference. Tomorrow you might. In ten years, you will. Ask yourself: Is the brain wiring I'm building one of distraction and reactivity—or of clarity and presence?

FROM THE ROAD NOT TAKEN TO THE ROAD YOU INTENTIONALLY CHOOSE

Have you ever felt the peace and clarity of a mindfulness retreat—only to watch it fade away as soon as real life resumes? You come back inspired, centered, and full of purpose, but within days, the noise of daily life and endless responsibilities starts to take over again. The calm dissolves, and what once felt permanent suddenly feels like a passing moment. You are not alone. I have met countless brilliant people—professionals, creators, and spiritual seekers—who have mastered their outer worlds yet struggle to sustain mindful living in the long run. Some begin with enthusiasm but give up too soon. Others practice correctly but without uniqueness or personal connection. And some simply have not found the approach that resonates deeply enough to last. Their question is always the same: *Why does mindfulness feel temporary?* That question led me to reflect deeply. Why do some people's mindfulness practices fade while others seem to live effortlessly in awareness?

The truth is, most of us have been relying only on temporary solutions—retreat highs, weekend workshops, expensive vacations, or inspirational books that stay beautifully unread on our shelves. Even when we do practice, we often miss the deeper connection: how to live mindfully every day, naturally, and permanently, regardless of what's happening around us. When I say **"permanent mindful living,"** I don't mean forever in an absolute sense—because nothing in life truly is. What I mean is a *lasting way of being* that stays with you through most of your life's journey—a practice so seamlessly integrated that it becomes second nature.

In this section, I discuss a living framework that helps you make mindfulness a *natural part of your existence.* The following are unique, experience-driven steps designed to help you sustain mindful living with minimal effort—steps that align with your rhythm, not against it. These practices don't promise tangible rewards like wealth or status. Instead, they offer something subtler but infinitely more powerful: an inner shift. A change in thought patterns, motivation, and perception that quietly transforms your everyday life into a mindful experience. The goal is simple yet profound—to help you reach a point where mindfulness is no longer something you *do*, but something you *are.* In the pages ahead, explore steps that lead you there—steps that work whether you're beginning your journey or trying to return to it. These are not momentary fixes. They are pathways to permanence. So take a breath, slow down, and prepare to explore what might just be the missing link in your mindful living journey.

Let's begin with the first step...

Step 1: Realization, Acceptance, and Positivity

The human world is demanding — one that constantly asks things of us. Some demands are circumstantial, some implied, and some come from love. And often, you can't say no to these demands because they come from people who mean the most to you. You find yourself caught in a loop where the days blur, the calendar keeps turning, and there's hardly a moment left for yourself. Forget mindful living — sometimes you can't even find time for basic things like skincare or reading a newspaper. Think about it: maybe you're taking care of a terminally ill family member all by yourself, or working multiple jobs just to make ends meet. Maybe you're so exhausted after a long day that all you can think about is getting seven hours of sleep. The truth is, life's responsibilities can feel endless. So amidst all this, how do you begin to practice mindful living — or better yet, make it a natural part of your daily life?

It begins with Realization.

Realization

Realization is the first and most essential step toward learning or practicing anything outside your comfort zone. Even if you haven't yet acted on it, if a genuine realization stirs within you — one that isn't just a passing thought, self-pity, or humorous remark — then you are already on the right path.

True realization comes from within. Others can inspire you, influence you, or plant a seed of thought, but the moment of awakening happens in silence — through observation, reflection, and honest awareness.

When it comes to mindful living, realization often begins quietly. You may have felt it before — a fleeting awareness that something needs to change — but it got buried under work or routine. Yet if that awareness stayed, even as a whisper, it's a sign that the process has already begun. Hold on it next time and note down on paper whatever you are feeling on a mobile or anywhere where you can find it later.

Acceptance

Once realization sets in, the next step naturally follows: Acceptance.

You need to accept that the responsibilities you carry will, at times, disrupt your life — and that's okay. You need to accept that mindful living isn't something to *attain* — it's something to *integrate* into your existing life, slowly and naturally, regardless of your situation. The pace may vary, and that too is okay.

You also need to recognize that much of your disconnection and self-pity stems from conditioning — the beliefs instilled by society, media, schools, and the environment you grew up in. This conditioning often teaches us to constantly do more, achieve more, and rarely pause for ourselves. But if you continue to live this way, you might have everything and still feel lost.

So, change — not by fighting or boasting about it — but by taking small, consistent steps. And believe me when I say this: no one can truly claim they don't have time for mindful living.

Even those who say so are likely already performing mindful acts unconsciously — just without awareness. You don't need hours; even ten minutes a day can make a difference.

Acceptance also requires shedding layers of ego — the "I'm too busy," "I already do enough," or "I know this" mindset. Only through acceptance can true learning begin. You need to accept your situation — whatever its cause — and understand that complaining or posting about it won't help.

True mindfulness isn't about showcasing your practice online. It's about doing it quietly, sincerely, when no one is watching. Accept your truth. Accept your surroundings. Accept your limitations and your strengths. Accept that society has conditioned you to look outward more than inward.

And remind yourself: if you are fulfilling your basic duties and not harming anyone, taking fifteen minutes a day to care for your inner self is not selfish — it's necessary.

We all have a role to play — for ourselves and for others — and it's only through mindful action that we can restart and renew. There may be months when you can't engage in any mindful activity, and that's alright too. What matters is that you always return to it.

Positivity

Now comes the most vital layer — Positivity.

Give yourself some space, as you give to others in today's era.

"Positivity is a deliberate art, but it is not about achieving the impossible state of a silent, doubt-free mind. Biologically, your brain is wired for survival, not constant bliss; due to the evolutionary 'negativity bias,' your subconscious will always scan for threats and generate doubts to keep you safe. Trying to completely eradicate negative thoughts is a battle against your own biology. Instead, the true practice lies in neuroplasticity—the understanding that while you cannot stop the automatic inflow of negativity, you *can* consciously build and strengthen positive neural pathways until they outnumber the negative ones. It is not about forcing the darkness out, but about turning up the light so brightly that the inevitable doubts no longer control your actions. Success, then, is not the absence of fear, but the ability to remain productive and peaceful even while your survival instincts try to tell you otherwise." And for those already practicing mindfulness: remember, it's okay to not feel okay sometimes, miss a meditation, feel negative for a few hours, miss a prayer, or a reflective moment. You don't have to fall into frustration or guilt. Simply realize, accept, and restart. You're human — and for anything lasting to take root, you must take breaks instead of quitting. Ultimately, the interplay of Realization, Acceptance, and Positivity becomes the foundation of permanent mindful living. When these three coexist in your life, mindfulness stops being an activity — it becomes your way of being.

Pause and Reflect: A Short Exercise

Take a few minutes right now — no rush, no pressure — and sit somewhere you feel comfortable. Let this be your moment of stillness. Then reflect on these questions in your mind or journal:

Realization: What part of your life feels most disconnected from peace right now? What quiet realization has been whispering to you, waiting to be heard?

Acceptance: What truth about your current situation are you resisting? How might your life shift if you simply accepted it without judgment?

Positivity: What is one small, positive habit — something you truly enjoy — that you can commit to for just ten minutes a day this week?

Breathe deeply. Let your answers come naturally, without overthinking. This is not about perfection — it's about presence.

When you finish, remind yourself gently:

"I am learning to realize, I am learning to accept, and I am choosing to live positively."

Carry that thought with you into the next step of your mindful journey.

Step 2: Not Just 21 Days — Give More to Your Habit

They say Rome wasn't built in a day — and neither did Shah Rukh Khan earn his first hit film or his Madame Tussauds statue overnight. Yet, in today's fast-paced world, we've begun to romanticize the idea that forming a habit takes exactly 21 days.

Media and Its Mirage

It's everywhere — articles, videos, challenges — all promising transformation in three short weeks. Sure, there's science behind it, but let's pause for a moment and reflect. If our DNA, brain, and personalities can vary so vastly, why wouldn't habit formation vary too?

So, if you haven't mastered your new habit in 21 days, it doesn't mean you've failed. It simply means you're human. Your timeline is your own.

Don't let the world convince you to quit just because your progress doesn't fit within a number. You might take two months, or even six, and that's perfectly fine. The point is not *how long* it takes — it's that you *keep going*. Because you are not a lab experiment or a rat in a cage being trained to respond to a signal. You are a human being — with a mind capable of will, determination, and resilience — something no science can quantify or define.

Let Science Fail You Occasionally, Even When It's Not Meant To

Think about it: have you ever heard anyone measure love, motivation, or compassion in kilograms or quintals? "Ten kilograms of motivation" or "seven quintals of love" — it sounds absurd, doesn't it? Then how can every human being, living in different environments, with different responsibilities, emotional capacities, and circumstances, be expected to build a habit in exactly 21 days?

Unless we all lived in the same controlled environment, it's impossible. So, while being aware of scientific studies is good, don't let numbers limit your potential.

Human nature is far too complex and beautiful to be bound by timelines. As Shakespeare spoke of the *seven stages of life* and philosophers of the *seven deadly sins*, we, too, are layered beings filled with desires and contradictions. We are biologically designed to want — and that's not wrong. What matters is how we channel those desires into conscious action.

Habits, Humans and Heart

Building a habit, especially one aligned with mindful living, takes time, patience, and deliberate effort. It's a slow sculpting of your mind — a process that may test your discipline but will reward you with something far greater than success: peace.

Peace is the true currency of good habits — the quiet joy that comes when your actions and intentions align. And that peace is what turns temporary habits into permanent mindfulness.

We can't eliminate desires, pleasures, or distractions. They're part of being human. But we can choose discipline — not as a punishment, but as a conscious act of love toward ourselves and others. Discipline, when born from awareness, doesn't restrict you — it frees you.

Keep acting. Keep doing. Keep showing up, even when you don't feel like it. One day, your consistent efforts will quietly evolve into effortless habits — habits that serve your peace and your purpose.

Because habits aren't formed by counting days;

they're formed by counting moments of awareness.

So start — even if it's imperfect, inconsistent, or awkward at first. Just start.

Your body might resist at the beginning; it's a slave to routine and comfort. But your mind — your greatest weapon — holds the power to shape, refine, and direct that body.

And when you start enjoying the results of your habits — the calm, the clarity, the steadiness — you'll no longer ask how many days it took. You'll simply know: *it was worth every one of them.*

Pause and Reflect: The Ripple Habit Exercise

"Every drop creates a ripple — but only the ripples that return to the center form a pattern."

This is not a habit tracker. It's a *habit mirror* — an inward exercise that allows you to watch how your actions ripple through your days.

Here's how you do it:

Name Your Drop:

Choose one small mindful habit you wish to form. It could be journaling for five minutes, drinking water with awareness, walking without your phone, or even taking three conscious breaths every morning. Write it down.

Mark Your Ripples:

For seven days, don't measure *whether you did it perfectly* — instead, note *how it made you feel afterward.*

Example:

"I felt calmer."

"I forgot once, but I noticed my mind was kinder to me."

"I didn't want to do it, but I did — and that gave me quiet pride."

Find the Return:

At the end of each week, ask yourself:

Did this habit return peace to me?

Did it ripple into other areas of my life — my patience, focus, or gratitude?

If it didn't, how can I adjust it so it does?

Expand the Circle:

After a month, add one more mindful habit — but only after the first has become effortless. Let it expand naturally, not forcefully, like ripples growing on still water.

The Ripple Habit Exercise teaches that it's not the number of days that matters — it's the number of times you return to your center. Every return strengthens the pattern. Every pause deepens the permanence.

So, let your ripples grow patiently.

And one day, you'll notice: the habit is no longer something you do — it's something you *are*.

Step 3. Follow The Integrated Path to Presence: Bridging Ancient Wisdom and Digital Immersion

Ancient Era and Mindfulness

Mindfulness is not a trend of our time; it is a wisdom carried across centuries, rooted in the quiet depths of Buddhism and Hinduism. Yet as the world around us transforms—through climate change, crowded cities, polluted air, buzzing gadgets, and constant movement—our ways of practicing mindfulness must adapt too. Still, its essence remains the same: a journey inward to understand ourselves, to observe life with clarity, to heal emotionally and physically, and to harmonize body, senses, and spirit. Nature has always been our greatest ally in this journey. Its silence, its fresh air, its unhurried rhythms teach mindfulness without a single word. But as access to nature becomes harder for many, virtual reality has emerged as a modern doorway—an artificial yet helpful bridge—allowing beginners to step into calming landscapes, guided by gentle voices and immersive visuals. Studies show that VR can help new practitioners start on the right path, offering structure and support in a world filled with noise.

Yet wisdom reminds us of another truth: the deepest introspection, the quiet handling of difficult emotions, often blossoms through traditional practices. Yoga, meditation, Vipassana, sound therapy—these are not relics of the past but living traditions that cannot be replaced. The future lies not in choosing between the old and the new, but in weaving them together. Ancient roots and modern technologies can coexist, creating a richer, more inclusive path to mindfulness for every age and every kind of seeker.

Amalgamation of Traditional and Modern

The contemporary path to mindful living requires a sophisticated synthesis that integrates the depth of ancient wisdom with the accessibility of modern technology. Recognizing that the digital age has drastically shortened attention spans and increased environmental chaos, tools like Virtual Reality (VR) function as a "skillful means," providing a fully immersive, distraction-free environment that is scientifically proven to improve focus and mental well-being for beginners.[1] To overcome the initial struggle of habit formation, structured programs, often incorporating techniques like NLP or rooted in established models like MBSR, offer the necessary *extrinsic motivation* to kickstart the journey and establish a routine.

However, it is crucial that individuals exercise ethical due diligence when selecting these programs and, more importantly, consciously transition from relying on mentors and external incentives toward *intrinsic motivation*—a sense of autonomy and personal competence—for sustained practice.[5] The ideal balance is achieved through the smart use of technology (as an anchor, not a distraction) to integrate micro-mindfulness habits into daily life, while reserving dedicated time for deep, non-digital practices like yoga or seated meditation, navigating the thin line of potential drawbacks like cybersickness or over-reliance. Because no headset can truly replace the feeling of real wind on our skin, the rise and fall of intentional breathing, the grounding weight of a straight, steady posture, or the healing presence of the natural world. VR may support us in a changing climate and an ever-rushing world, but it should never push nature aside. Let technology be an aid—not an escape. Because at the heart of mindfulness lies a simple truth: presence begins where we are, not in the devices we hold.

Pause & Reflect:

When was the last time I spent time outside without documenting, measuring, or multitasking?

What emotions surface when I leave my phone behind — discomfort, relief, emptiness, curiosity?

Step 4: Follow Multidisciplinary Approach In all Areas of Life

Science isn't just for laboratories, research papers, or white coats.

It's for *life*.

Too often, we believe that only a doctor should know about human psychology or that only a marketer needs to understand consumer behavior. But, my friend, that belief limits you. Because in truth, science belongs to everyone who wants to understand life more deeply. I'm not asking you to become a doctor or a calorie-obsessed fitness enthusiast. I'm inviting you to become an *observer* of your own system. Learn about your brain, your hormones, and your nervous system. Understand why your mind drifts or your emotions swing. These are not abstract ideas — they're everyday realities shaping your behavior, your focus, and your peace. Science shouldn't just invent tools to make our lives faster — it should help us understand ourselves better. With today's sophisticated technology, it's easier than ever to learn how your brain, body, and emotions function. The key is to use science as a *compass*, not a *crutch* — as a means to guide your self-awareness, not justify your impulses.

Science and Your Daily Life

Science can help you see what's happening *within* you, not just around you. It can explain why you react, why you crave, why you resist, and why certain patterns repeat in your behavior. When used consciously, it becomes a mirror — helping you read your mind's language with greater clarity. For example, did you know that yoga is actually a science — the science of the mind-body connection? Rooted in ancient Indian philosophy, yoga has evolved into a practice that's now studied by modern researchers for its measurable effects on physical, emotional, and neurological well-being. It teaches you to read the language of your body — its signals, tensions, and subtle messages — long before illness or imbalance takes hold.

This is what science, in its purest form, does: it helps you *see.*
To see patterns before they become problems.
To understand reactions before they become regrets.
To interpret emotions before they turn into storms.

Reality Checks and Reading

Take the example of alcohol. Many see it as a harmless form of relaxation or coping mechanism — a glass of wine after a long day. But science tells a different story. Research from Harvard Medical School and Johns Hopkins reveals that even small, regular consumption of alcohol alters neurotransmitters like GABA and dopamine, impairing cognitive control, focus, and emotional balance. It dulls the prefrontal cortex — the brain's center for decision-making and attention — which is the very foundation of mindfulness. Oxford studies have shown that alcohol's sedative effects blur presence, weakening the brain's capacity for sustained attention and self-awareness. Further studies by the University of Maryland School of Medicine and the University of Michigan found that consistent alcohol intake — even a few times a week — accelerates brain aging. It might offer temporary relief from stress, but over time, it diminishes clarity and resilience. These findings aren't just data points — they're lessons in mindfulness. Understanding the *why* behind your habits builds conscious choice. When you recognize the biological consequences of a behavior, you begin to act not from guilt, but from awareness. That's when true transformation begins. And this principle applies far beyond alcohol.

A Multidisciplinary Approach for Yourself—Not Just Your Business"

Reading, observing, and implementing insights from disciplines like psychology, behavioral science, neuroscience, sociology, or even astrology and geology can help you understand your moods, emotions, reactions, and habits. These fields, when approached with curiosity, offer practical wisdom about how we function and why we feel what we feel. So, read deeply. Learn from authentic sources. Listen to your body as much as your books. The more you understand the mechanics of your mind and body, the more naturally mindfulness will grow in you — not as a belief, but as a lived experience. Whether it's your health, relationships, personal growth, or the way you manage your team — everyday science can guide you toward greater awareness and balance. You don't need a PhD or complex formulas to use it. Even basic principles can illuminate your mind in remarkable ways.

🙞 Pause and Reflect: The Inner Scientist Practice (Original Method)

"Science begins with curiosity — not in a lab, but in the heart that asks *why*."

This exercise helps you reconnect with the *observer within you* — the calm scientist who studies life not to control it, but to understand it.

Here's how to begin:
Observe Without Labeling:

For one entire day, treat your mind and body as a gentle experiment.

Notice your thoughts, energy shifts, hunger patterns, mood changes — but resist labeling them as "good" or "bad." Simply collect the data.

Find the Triggers:
Ask yourself once in the morning and once before bed:
What triggered my calm today?
What disturbed it?
What repeated itself?
Connect the Dots:
At the end of the day, reflect for 5 minutes.

Can you find any pattern between your food, your sleep, your emotions, and your focus?

You don't need conclusions — just awareness. That's your first scientific finding.

Name One Discovery:

Write one sentence that begins with "Today, I understood that…"

This small line is your *research summary*. It trains your mind to learn from living, not just reading.

Do this once or twice a week — not to analyze yourself endlessly, but to understand your rhythm. Over time, you'll find that awareness naturally shapes behavior.

And when science meets mindfulness within you, understanding replaces control — and peace replaces effort.

STEP5.Taming the Inferno Within: On the Virtue of Restraint

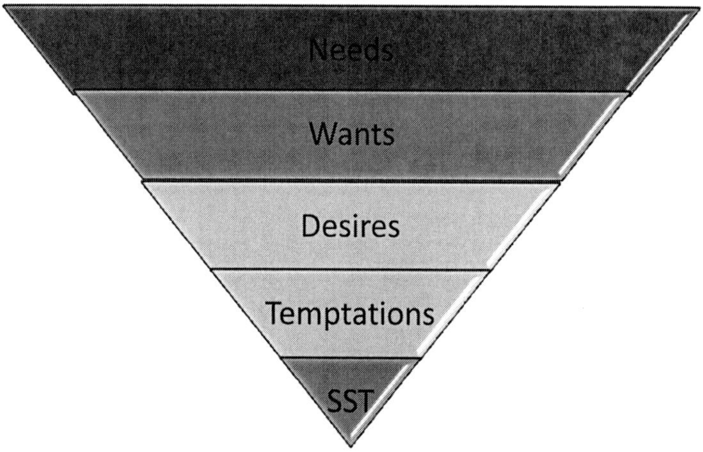

SST — Standards and Conditioning by Society and Surroundings

Most people are familiar with the simple diagram that separates Needs, Wants, and Desires. We've seen it in psychology classes, in textbooks, or floating somewhere on the internet. But that diagram has always been incomplete. There is a fourth and fifth layer hovering above it—a layer we rarely notice but constantly live under:

Mindfulness begins by recognizing this invisible layer.

The Art of Saying No — To Temptation Before It Turns Into Habit

Dante once wrote about souls trapped in the circles of hell, not because someone condemned them, but because their own desires swallowed them whole. Their suffering was self-created—an echo of every moment they said "yes" when a gentle "no" could have saved them.

Standards & Conditioning by Society.

This layer shapes how we think, what we aim for, what we buy, and even how we see ourselves. It doesn't shout. It whispers. It seeps into us through comparisons, trends, expectations, and the quiet pressure to "keep up." Most of us don't realize that half our desires aren't born inside us—they're borrowed from the world around us.

Our world today isn't very different.

Temptations aren't hidden anymore. They shine from screens, knock on our phones, and appear at our doorsteps within minutes. With one swipe or click, desire becomes delivery.

Instant everything has eroded a quality the older generation held dearly: the ability to wait. And once waiting disappears, craving grows. There is no harm in pleasure. There is harm in losing yourself to it.

Mindfulness is the art of pausing right before the yes—of listening to the small voice inside that asks, *"Is this what I truly want, or what I'm conditioned to want?"*

Needs, Wants, Desires — and the Hidden Fourth Layer

Let's revisit the famous pyramid, but through a mindful lens:

Needs — The essentials that anchor your survival and emotional well-being. Wants — Comforts that add color, convenience, and ease. Desires — Aspirations born from imagination and longing, often connected to identity. Society's Standards — The silent layer shaping what we believe we should need, want, or desire. A mindful person sees this fourth layer clearly.

Most people never do.

Modern life blurs the lines between all three inner layers. A want begins to look like a need. A desire begins to feel urgent. And society's standards slip in quietly, telling us that happiness requires more, newer, faster, better.

But "better" is a moving target. You chase it, and it keeps moving. You reach it, and it shifts again. This constant chase pulls us away from ourselves—away from the quiet space where clarity actually lives.

The Loop of Endless Upgrade

Many people today live on repeat:
Wake up → Earn → Buy → Upgrade → Repeat.
Without mindfulness, this loop feels normal.
With mindfulness, it suddenly feels exhausting.

This is the modern version of Dante's circles—endless striving, endless hunger, endless comparison. Souls chasing shadows, forgetting the ground beneath their feet.

An unmindful life is noisy.

A mindful life is spacious.

The Wisdom of Earlier Generations

If you look back—not far, just one or two generations—you'll notice something quietly beautiful. They lived with less, yet felt more. Choices were fewer, but clarity was clearer. They didn't question their worth each morning through screens. They didn't feel the need to upgrade their lives every weekend. Their hearts were not constantly interrupted by pings.

They cherished what they had. They moved toward their dreams slowly, steadily, without the weight of comparison.

Read Dante. Read Shakespeare. Read Kalidasa's *Meghadūta*. Read the life of Dr. A.P.J. Abdul Kalam.

You'll find the same pattern in all of them:

ambition without restlessness, desire without desperation, progress without losing self.

They were hungry—but hungry for knowledge, purpose, and meaning. Their minds were full, even when their pockets weren't. Their inner world was wealth enough.

Mindfulness teaches us to return to this inner richness.

Needs, Desires, Temptations — A Mindful Distinction

A mindful life rests on understanding three truths:

Needs to bring balance.

Desires bring direction.

Temptations bring distraction.

The problem isn't that temptations exist.

The problem is that we rarely notice when temptation replaces desire, and desire replaces need. With awareness, the lines become clear again.

Mindfulness is simply the art of seeing.

Pause and Reflect:

A Simple Mindfulness Exercise

Take a notebook.

Write down the temptations you often give in to—not to judge yourself, but to meet yourself.

Notice which ones come from genuine joy.
Notice which ones come from habit.
Notice which ones come from insecurity.
Notice which ones come from society's standards, not your own values.

This small act of awareness breaks the loop.

Mindfulness does not ask you to give up everything.

It only asks you to wake up to what truly adds value—and what quietly takes it away.

When you begin to see clearly, the pyramid becomes simple again. Needs remain needs. Wants to stay gentle. Desires become purposeful. And temptations lose their grip.

And in that clarity, you finally return home—to yourself.

Everyday Temptations: The Coffee and the Cart

Example 1: The Coffee Temptation

Imagine you start every morning with an expensive café latte. At first, it feels harmless—a small ritual, a moment of pleasure, a reward you think you deserve. But slowly, without noticing, it shifts. What began as a treat becomes something you *depend* on. You don't crave the coffee; you crave the comfort of indulgence.

One day, you choose to make your coffee at home.
Not to save money.
Not to "discipline" yourself.

But simply to take back control.

Something subtle shifts inside you. You feel lighter, more intentional, more in charge. That small "no" becomes the beginning of something larger. You realize it was never about coffee—it was about reclaiming your choices.

Every time you resist an unnecessary temptation, your clarity sharpens. Your self-respect strengthens. You remind yourself: you are in charge—not your cravings, not your habits, not society's expectations.

Example 2: The Shopping Temptation

Consider another common pattern: online shopping. You're not unhappy. You're not lacking anything. But an ad pops up. A sale appears. A friend posts a picture with something new.

Suddenly, your mind whispers, *"Maybe I need this too."*

You add things to your cart—clothes, gadgets, accessories—items that promise excitement, confidence, or improvement. For a moment, the purchase feels thrilling. But the feeling fades quickly, leaving behind clutter, guilt, or the urge to buy again.

One day, you pause before clicking "Buy Now."

You take a breath.

You ask yourself, *"Do I really want this, or do I just want the feeling it gives me?"*

The answer surprises you.
You close the tab.
You feel a strange, quiet victory—

the kind that money can't buy.

That single "no" creates space—space in your mind, your home, and your inner world. It becomes a reminder that real satisfaction doesn't come from adding more things, but from needing fewer.

Mindfulness: The Strength to Say No

Mindfulness is often misunderstood. It's not limited to meditation, silence, soft music, or sitting cross-legged on a mountain. You don't need to distance yourself from society or give up modern life. Mindfulness isn't about escaping the world.

Mindfulness is about living fully conscious inside the world—right in the middle of noise, choices, temptations, and distractions.

It means learning to say no, not just to other people, but to yourself:

To the small urges,
The sudden cravings,
The impulses that feel harmless,
The temptations that promise joy but drain your peace.
Real mindfulness cannot grow in a mind that obeys every impulse.
It needs space.
It needs awareness.
It needs the strength to pause before reacting.

True mindfulness blooms when you can stay centered in the middle of chaos—not outside it. Real growth happens not on serene mountaintops, but right here, in the ordinary rush of your everyday life. You don't become mindful by escaping challenges; you become mindful by meeting them with awareness.

Every "no" you say to temptation is actually a "yes":
a yes to peace,
a yes to balance,
a yes to your best self.

And when you start choosing from awareness rather than impulse, something beautiful happens—

you begin to return home to yourself.

Pause and Reflect:

"Control feels safe, but trust builds peace."

✦ Are you giving others the space to learn and evolve on their own?

✦ What could you do with the energy you currently spend on micromanaging?

Step 6. Practice Actual Minimalism

#Minimalism # Aesthetic

Minimalism is a word that has become incredibly popular in recent years—but what most people practice is often far from *actual* minimalism. There's a big difference between *looking* minimalistic and *living* minimalistically. Actual minimalism is quiet. It's not about curated white spaces or perfect aesthetic feeds on social media. It's about living with genuine intention—showing less, doing more, and finding peace in simplicity. True minimalism makes you a little uncomfortable at first because it challenges your habits, not just your possessions. It teaches you to buy less, post less, and focus more on what truly adds value to your life. Real minimalism is *practical* and *sustainable*. It doesn't demand that you throw away half your home or follow an influencer's checklist—it asks for small, conscious shifts. Reuse what you already have. Simplify your routines. Eat cleaner, move more, sleep better. It's less about products and more about *presence*. In a world shaped by Japanese philosophies, Korean routines, American dreams, and Indian epics, many of us have spent years absorbing wisdom from every corner of the globe. And then came COVID—an unexpected teacher that forced us to pause. Suddenly, life slowed down. Our priorities shifted. We discovered that we could live with far less than we ever imagined. We became mindful of waste, mindful of time, mindful of breath. For a moment, the world practiced minimalism together.

But as the world reopened, something curious happened. While some people carried their newfound awareness into everyday life, many slipped into a different kind of minimalism—one that was curated rather than cultivated. A sort of *show-it-off minimalism.* Homes staged for Instagram, capsule wardrobes built for attention, "slow living" performed for the camera. Happy selfies, soft sunlight, muted tones—beautiful, yes, but not the heart of the practice.

Actual Minimalism

True minimalism isn't aesthetic; it's internal. It's not about how little you own, but how deeply you understand yourself. It begins with acknowledging your physical and mental limitations, exploring the roots of your habits, finding gentle solutions, and slowly weaving them into your daily routine. It is quiet work—silent, steady, and deeply personal. It's the habit you maintain not just on vacation or during a social detox, but on a regular Monday morning when nobody is watching.

And here's something many people miss: minimalism isn't just about decluttering your home—it's also about decluttering your *mind.* It's about silencing mental noise, letting go of emotional baggage, and curbing that constant desire to buy or compare.

Sadly, minimalism has also become a trend to *show off.* People post "before-and-after" photos of their wardrobes and call it a lifestyle. But true minimalism doesn't need applause. It's not about how it looks—it's about how it *feels.* It's a quiet decision to choose peace over possessions, quality over quantity, and clarity over chaos.

Minimalism, at its core, is mindfulness. It invites us to reduce the noise outside so we can hear the truth inside. It teaches us to choose intention over impulse, presence over performance, and alignment over appearance. When practiced sincerely, it stops being a lifestyle trend and becomes a way of being—a commitment to living with clarity, compassion, and purpose.

And the beauty of it all? No selfie can capture that. Only life can.

Try this: start small. Declutter one corner of your home, or delete ten unnecessary apps from your phone. As you do, notice how you feel. Minimalism isn't a weekend project—it's a daily practice of letting go, little by little.

Pause and Reflect:

"Minimalism isn't about having less. It's about making room for more—more peace, more purpose, and more presence."

✦ Ask yourself: *What am I holding onto—physically or emotionally—that no longer serves me?*

✦ What would my life look like if I stopped trying to impress and started trying to simplify?

WHAT WE OFTEN FORGET TO REMEMBER

Here are a few truths that don't need to be taught — only recalled. Consider this a soft nudge back to what you already know in your heart.

The Gift of Doing Nothing: Staying Bored on Purpose

We live in a world that glorifies busyness. Capitalism has sold us the idea that if we're not working, producing, or improving ourselves every minute, we're wasting time. Productivity is valuable—but being obsessed with constant productivity is exhausting and unnatural.

Think of it this way: if you ate your favorite burger every single day, how long before it stopped feeling like a treat? Even pleasure loses meaning without pause. The same applies to your mind—it needs time to rest and wander.

So yes, I'm asking you to do something that sounds absurd at first: get bored.

Once or twice a week, set aside an hour to do absolutely nothing. No phone, no scrolling, no mental checklist. Just sit quietly—on your balcony, in your favorite chair, or under a tree. Sip tea if you want to, but resist the urge to *do so*. Let your thoughts come and go without judgment.

When you first try this, it may feel uncomfortable. Your mind will race with random thoughts, your hand will reach for your phone, and you'll want to get up. That's normal. But if you stay with it, something magical happens—your mind begins to relax. You stop reacting and start observing. You start hearing yourself again.

Constant stimulation—notifications, emails, streaming, noise—keeps your brain in a state of low-grade anxiety. "Doing nothing" is not laziness; it's mental detox. It allows your brain to reset, your emotions to settle, and your creativity to bloom.

Watch a tiger in the wild—it spends most of its time sitting silently, observing. When it finally moves, it's focused, fast, and precise. Stillness sharpens awareness. Humans aren't so different. By learning to sit still, even for twenty minutes, you train your mind to find calm within chaos.

Try it this week: take a deliberate "boredom break." Sit quietly with no purpose, no productivity goals. Let yourself just *be.* You might discover that boredom is not emptiness—it's space.

🕊 Mindful Insight

"In a world that rewards constant motion, stillness is a quiet rebellion."

✦ Can you spend 20 minutes doing absolutely nothing—no phone, no chores, no guilt?

✦ What thoughts or emotions arise when you sit still? Observe them without judging.

JUST START …

Cultivating self-awareness without judgment and making conscious decisions are deeply connected parts of mindful living. When you observe your thoughts, emotions, cravings, and habits with kindness instead of criticism, you create space to respond rather than react. This same awareness is what strengthens your ability to make decisions with clarity instead of fear or impulse. Every choice—whether changing a job, picking a new hobby, or simply deciding how to spend your evening—carries energy and shapes your life. The moment you choose with intention, you stop living on autopilot and start reclaiming your direction. Decision-making isn't always easy; it's messy, uncomfortable, and full of second-guessing, just like learning any new skill. But the more you practice making small, mindful choices, the stronger your inner stability becomes. Mindfulness helps you see before you choose, guiding you toward what truly feels right rather than what the world says. Just like you sometimes feel conscious in a particular outfit but still choose to wear it until you grow confident in it, think of your body AND MIND the same way. Treat it with awareness, care, and patience—not just on the outside but internally too. When you nurture it from within, you naturally start feeling better in your own skin. External fixes like tummy belts may hide things temporarily, but you always know what's real. True comfort comes from tending to your body lovingly, not masking it. To build awareness, you may feel nervous or confused at first, but take it one day and one conscious choice at a time—let the results reveal themselves naturally. Expects. Over time, this gentle awareness and intentional decision-making lead to better judgment, emotional resilience, and a sense of ownership over your life. Mindful living doesn't begin with perfect meditation—it begins with choosing to live consciously, one small decision at a time.

Breaking the Mechanical Loop: Stepping Off the Hamster Wheel

With rising living costs, social pressures, and constant digital noise, many of us have become part of an invisible machine—waking up, working, scrolling, sleeping, and repeating. Even if you manage to fit in a gym session, it still feels like you're running in circles rather than moving forward.

This is what I call *the mechanical loop*—a pattern of survival dressed up as living.

And here's the irony: even when we take breaks, we often fill them with stimulation—vacations, photos, content, constant motion. But rest doesn't always mean going somewhere far. Sometimes, taking a paid leave and spending it at home—without guilt—can be the most rejuvenating act of all.

We've forgotten the joy of doing small, ordinary things slowly. We've forgotten that negative emotions—sadness, boredom, even mild frustration—are not enemies to avoid but signals to listen to. When you refuse to sit with discomfort, it doesn't disappear; it simply hides and resurfaces later in more harmful ways.

Taking even *10–15 minutes out of your mechanical loop* every day can make a difference. Sit quietly, go for a walk, water your plants, or just breathe without checking your phone. Don't live like a pauper, denying yourself every comfort—but don't chase the illusion of living like a king every day either. Balance is the real luxury.

And ask yourself: are you *experiencing* life, or merely *documenting* it for others to see? Because no amount of likes can replace a moment truly lived.

Pause and Reflect:

"You're not a machine; you're a rhythm. Learn when to move, when to pause, and when to simply *be*."

✦ What's one small thing you can stop doing on autopilot today?

✦ Can you permit yourself to rest without feeling guilty?

Building a Complementary Value System: Mindfulness Needs a Backbone

If humans were meant to live in isolation, we'd be designed differently—one hand, one leg, one eye. But nature made us *in pairs* for a reason: to cooperate, to balance, to complement. The same principle applies to life itself. Nothing meaningful thrives single-handedly.

Yet today's culture glorifies hyper-independence. We're told we can "do it all alone," that asking for help is weakness, that solitude equals strength. But if you look closely, even those who live "independently" depend on others—a farmer grows their food, engineers build their roads, delivery workers bring their essentials. Interdependence isn't a flaw of humanity; it's its beauty.

Mindfulness, too, cannot exist in isolation. It flourishes when grounded in a strong *value system.* Without values like kindness, curiosity, wonder, and wisdom, mindfulness becomes a hollow ritual—a performance rather than a practice.

So, while you meditate, reflect, and slow down, also nurture your internal compass. Read something that inspires moral reflection. Engage in meaningful conversations. Observe nature with curiosity. Appreciate people's differences. Some values are innate, others can be developed—but all of them deepen your mindfulness.

Because ultimately, awareness without values is like sight without direction—you can see everything and still be lost.

Pause and Reflect:

"Mindfulness is the flower; your values are the soil."

✦ Which values do you consciously live by each day?

✦ How can you bring curiosity, empathy, or wisdom into a simple daily act?

Stop Monitoring Every Other Person: Teach, Trust, and Let Go

Imagine a teacher running behind one student all day, checking every answer, correcting every move. It sounds absurd, right? No teacher does that. They teach, take questions, and trust the students to practice. The same principle applies to life.

If you want to live mindfully, you need to release your obsession with control. Constantly monitoring your colleagues, children, or loved ones might give you a temporary illusion of order—but it drains your peace, fuels anxiety, and steals your time for self-awareness.

Whether at home or work, teach what you know, set boundaries, give feedback—and then let go. Everyone deserves space to make mistakes, learn, and grow at their own pace. Real leadership (and mindful living) means guiding without hovering.

Perfection is not the goal; growth is.

And yes, of course, there are exceptions—terminally ill family members or people who truly depend on you require closer attention. But even they need moments of space, dignity, and independence.

Try this mantra: Teach and leave. Guide and trust. Because when you stop over-monitoring others, you finally have the time and emotional space to monitor *yourself*.

Pause and Reflect:

"Every decision you make is a mirror of your awareness. The more mindful your choices, the more peaceful your life becomes."

✦ What's one small decision today that you can make more consciously?

✦ Do you often make choices out of fear or out of genuine intention?

Aspirational Inflation: When Dreams Start Costing Too Much

Recently, I came across a fascinating term in a finance book — *"Aspirational Inflation."* At first, I laughed and thought, *"Even inflation has an aspirational version now?"* But as I kept reading, I realized how accurately it captures the silent pressure many of us live under today.

Aspirational inflation refers to the gradual expansion of our desires as our income, exposure, or social circle grows. The more we earn or achieve, the more we start wanting — not out of need, but out of habit. The car that once felt luxurious now feels basic. The apartment that once brought joy suddenly feels small. Even holidays, clothes, or gadgets lose their charm faster than before.

And it's not entirely our fault. We live in a time where success is constantly redefined by what we *see*, not what we *feel.* Social media feeds, marketing algorithms, and even peer conversations subtly convince us that growth must always look visible — a newer phone, a better job title, a bigger trip, or a fancier lifestyle. This is how aspiration quietly turns into expectation, and contentment turns into comparison.

Now, understanding aspirational inflation is actually important. It's not a concept meant to make you guilty for wanting better things. Rather, it teaches you to prepare for life's changing financial realities with awareness — to budget, plan, and save without losing your peace of mind. Learning about it builds financial intelligence and foresight.

But the real lesson lies in *how* we respond to it. Preparing for aspirational inflation doesn't mean becoming obsessed with earning or hoarding. It means knowing when to stop chasing and start savoring. It's about distinguishing between genuine aspirations that add value to your life and artificial ones that only drain your joy.

Because here's the truth — your aspirations shouldn't be dictated by what society praises.

They should arise from what your soul values. A mindful person can still have goals, ambition, and dreams — but they pursue them with purpose, not pressure. They grow without letting their wants spiral out of control.

This is where mindfulness and decision-making intersect beautifully. When you live mindfully, you begin to see your desires for what they are — fleeting, often external, sometimes borrowed. You start making conscious choices about what truly matters, and in doing so, you free yourself from the endless treadmill of comparison.

The author of that finance book wasn't warning readers to stop dreaming — he was encouraging them to *think before they climb.* To grow thoughtfully, not recklessly. To upgrade not just their lifestyle, but also their awareness.

And maybe, that's what we all need today — a collective shift in mindset. It's not that governments, nonprofits, or businesses aren't trying to address issues of excess and imbalance — they are. But it's not enough. True change will only come when *we*, as individuals, start making mindful choices in our everyday lives. How we consume, how we shop, how we save, how we treat the planet — all of it matters.

We are already running late — for ourselves and for nature. But mindfulness gives us a chance to slow down, reset, and realign. It helps us remember that growth isn't about owning more; it's about needing less and living more consciously.

Pause and Reflect:

"Aspirations are beautiful when they inspire growth, not when they demand proof."

✦ Are your dreams truly your own — or a reflection of someone else's expectations?

✦ Can you redefine success as peace of mind, not a bigger price tag?

Combine Intention With Action

Mindful living begins by understanding that manifestation alone cannot replace consistent effort, careful planning, and practical execution. Wanting a goal—whether losing weight, becoming calmer, or improving your life—must be paired with disciplined habits such as movement, mindful eating, meditation, or structured routines. Just as owning a car does not guarantee maintenance unless you actively take care of it, starting any healing or transformation program only gives you a head start; the real progress depends on how responsibly you continue the work. Eco-therapies, NLP practices, or guided programs can initiate change, but they are not magic shortcuts. Without your personal participation—adjusting your behavior, making practical choices, and taking daily steps—manifestation becomes empty wishful thinking. Mindful living asks you to align your intentions with real-world actions so growth becomes steady, grounded, and achievable.

Practice Patience and Accept Individual Pace

Another essential aspect of mindful living is recognizing that change happens gradually and differently for everyone. You may not suddenly feel enlightened or transformed just because you started practicing mindfulness, meditation, or intentional habits. Progress can be slow, subtle, and influenced by many factors—your genetics, personality, lifestyle, diet, consistency, and emotional state. Two people doing the same practices, like mindful eating or yoga, may still experience different results, and that is completely normal. Mindful living teaches you not to obsess over outcomes, but to stay present with the process and allow change to unfold at its natural pace. Sometimes goals may shift or remain unachieved, and even that is part of the journey. What truly matters is noticing small improvements, remaining patient, and understanding that growth is not instant magic but a collection of tiny, steady steps that eventually reshape your life.

Stay Consistent with Small Daily Practices

Mindful living is built on small, repeated actions rather than occasional bursts of motivation. Even five minutes of meditation, pausing before meals, or taking conscious breaths throughout the day significantly influences your mindset over time. Consistency acts like gentle polishing—it slowly clears mental clutter and strengthens your focus. You don't need dramatic rituals or long routines; what matters is showing up regularly, even when you don't feel like it. These tiny habits accumulate and create long-term change, much like slow drops of water shaping stone. When you consistently bring awareness into daily activities—walking, eating, working, communicating—life becomes more intentional and less reactive. The key is not perfection but steady engagement, trusting that every mindful moment contributes to your overall well-being and clarity.

Remove the Myths of Multitasking

"Burnout." It's a word we hear almost every day—and for many of us, it's become normal. But one of the biggest reasons we feel exhausted isn't just long hours or heavy workloads—it's *multitasking*.

Somehow, we've started believing that doing many things at once means we're being productive. But if you really look closer, multitasking often leaves you mentally scattered, emotionally drained, and only half-present in everything you do.

People often tell me, "I multitask because I don't have time." But I've learned that doing more things doesn't always mean getting more done. Multitasking might help you move fast, but it rarely helps you move well. You may finish tasks—but at the cost of focus, creativity, and joy. It's like eating a delicious meal while constantly checking your phone—you never really *taste* it.

Science agrees. The human brain isn't designed for multitasking; it's built for focus. What we think is multitasking is actually rapid task-switching—your brain jumping between tasks and trying to reorient itself each time. That constant switching tires out your mental circuits and lowers your efficiency.

From a neuroscience point of view, multitasking strains three key brain networks:

The frontoparietal control network, which helps you set goals and make decisions.

The dorsal attention network, which keeps you focused.

The ventral attention network, which alerts you to distractions.

When all three are working overtime, your brain feels like a browser with too many tabs open—sluggish and overheated. That's why after a day of juggling tasks, even simple ones, you feel drained. Coffee can't fix that. Rest can, and so can *single-tasking.*

Instead of trying to do everything, try doing one thing with full attention. When you give a task your undivided focus, you do it better, faster, and with more satisfaction. The calm that follows is not just peace of mind—it's productivity reborn.

Try this: tomorrow, choose two priorities. Do them one at a time. Silence your notifications. Notice how your stress levels drop, and your energy lasts longer. You'll realize that focus, not frenzy, is where true efficiency lives.

💡 Mindful Insight

"Multitasking is the illusion of progress. Focus is the reality of growth."

✦ What's one area of your life where multitasking has cost you peace or quality?

✦ What would change if you gave each task your full, undivided attention—even for just one day?

Hacking Mental Health—Offline and Outdoors

With the world the way it is—wars raging, pollution rising, inequality growing, and even children under ten facing digital addictions—mental health can no longer be treated as an afterthought. It should already be part of every school curriculum, right alongside math and science. Instead of teaching only definitions, we should be helping young minds develop emotional intelligence, empathy, and community values—skills that actually build resilience.

But here's the truth: taking care of mental health doesn't always require therapy apps or expensive retreats or only theoretical knowledge. Sometimes, the most effective therapy is the simplest—*physical movement in the open air.* Breaking a sweat outdoors, especially in the lap of nature, is one of the most underrated mental health hacks.

Gyms are great for structured workouts, but they come with limitations—closed air systems, artificial lighting, recycled air, and the constant reflection of mirrors. You're often trapped in an environment that disconnects you from the natural world.

After your workout, you step into another controlled space—an air-conditioned office—and spend the rest of the day breathing filtered air, staring at screens. Physically, you may be training your body, but mentally, you're still boxed in.

Running in your neighborhood park, on the other hand, offers a different kind of medicine. You breathe fresh air, soak in sunlight, and hear real sounds instead of gym playlists. You greet neighbors, watch trees sway, and feel the uneven ground beneath your feet.

You reconnect—with your body, your breath, and your surroundings. These small moments of interaction build real happiness, not just fitness.

Of course, there are exceptions—cities with heavy pollution or extreme climates may make outdoor workouts difficult. But even then, finding small ways to connect with nature—a walk on your terrace, some morning stretches by an open window—can make a difference.

Nature heals what screens can't. When you move outdoors, you're not just exercising your body—you're resetting your mind.

Pause & Reflect

"Your body is meant to move, not just to perform. Let nature be your gym and sunlight your therapy."

✦ When was the last time you broke a sweat under the open sky?

✦ Can you swap one gym session this week for a mindful walk or jog outdoors?

Remember The Beautiful Dance of Yin and Yang: Chaos and Peace

The symbol of yin and yang has been one of my favorite symbols personally. You know why. Because it represents the true human nature, devoid of Flory decoration. Brutal, honest, and so much human. Imagine the Yin Yang not as a static symbol, but as the heartbeat of the universe, where opposing forces don't just clash—they dance.

It captures the eternal, swirling chase of light and darkness, reminding us that chaos and order are actually inseparable partners. The distinct black and white halves reveal a profound secret: inside every shadow lies a spark of light, and within every light, a seed of shadow. It serves as the ultimate reminder that you cannot have the mountaintop without the valley; existence is a beautiful, necessary tension.

This natural law of duality—the fact that light cannot exist without shadow—isn't just external; it defines us internally. You have to accept that both positive and negative energies, both 'good' and 'evil,' reside within us.

You can't expect to be at peace all the time, nor will your environment allow it.

Fighting this reality is where our inner friction begins.

Instead of fighting for constant serenity, your real work is figuring out how to anchor your sanity *amidst* the storm, or how to keep your productivity humming even when things feel messy.

This is the core of true self-mastery—not eliminating chaos, but mastering your mind within it. The reason this internal mastery is so crucial is that everything in life operates on a cycle. Remember the concept of the cycle: everything is cyclical! From the phases of the moon to our own emotions and energy levels. You can't maintain iron-clad control over yourself twenty-four hours a day.

While you can—and should—work on your mindset, boost your emotional awareness, and formulate great strategies, sometimes things will simply descend into chaos. You will lose your cool occasionally. And honestly? That's okay. This fluctuation is the natural pulse of life, not a personal failing.

Therefore, we must adjust our expectations of ourselves. Whether you study the lives of spiritual figures or everyday heroes, you see it plainly: good and evil, happiness and struggle, coexist. You can't 'hack' your happy hormones and be joyful all the time, and honestly, that wouldn't even be healthy! The pursuit of perpetual happiness is an exhausting, artificial goal that sets you up for inevitable failure and self-criticism.

This is where true acceptance begins: it is perfectly natural to cry for no reason when no one is watching, or to feel a deep sense of sadness that has no immediate cause.

It is okay to be unhappy sometimes, to feel restless, or to experience profound boredom. These are not flaws in your character or failures in your strategy; they are the basic, beautiful, and necessary textures of human emotion.

Trying to avoid or suppress these difficult feelings is not a solution—it's a fast track to mental rigidity and burnout. Instead, we must practice allowing them to surface, acknowledging their presence without judgment, and understanding the temporary nature of every state.

So, make sure you experience the full beauty of this entire spectrum. It's a gift unique to humankind. Animals feel, sure, but they operate only in happy or unhappy states; there is no nuanced middle ground for them.

If you want a brilliant, relatable illustration of this complexity, watch the animated movie *Inside Out*—it captures this concept perfectly. Embrace the whole messy, magnificent package of being human.

If you dive deep into religious texts or even just trace the journey of someone you truly admire, you'll quickly realize that their timeline wasn't a flat, peaceful line. It was a chart full of peaks and valleys, a constant flux between peace and utter chaos. No one gets to where they are overnight.

They, too, had to take breaks, prioritize family, deal with the sudden shock of an accident, or grieve the loss of a loved one.

Life happened. This is crucial to remember: their greatness wasn't defined by the *absence* of struggle, but by their reaction to it.

But the defining characteristic? They never truly quit. That resilience is what made all the difference. Chaos and peace are two sides of the same coin—a total Yin and Yang situation. Paste this symbol or look at it now and then to remind yourselves about your own nature.

Pause and Reflect:

Do I ever chase "purity" (being only good, only calm, only strong), and how does that affect my balance?

What might balance look like instead of perfection?

A FINAL NOTE

If you've reached this page, I want to take a moment to simply say—*thank you.*

Thank you for staying with me through these reflections, stories, and small awakenings. Writing this book was never about preaching perfection. It was about sharing a journey—mine, yours, and ours—as humans learning to pause, breathe, and live a little more consciously in a world that never stops moving.

Mindful living is not a trend. It's not about incense, rituals, or picture-perfect moments. It's about learning to find stillness in your own messy, ordinary, beautiful life. It's about accepting that you will sometimes fall off track—and that's perfectly okay. The point isn't to remain mindful every second, but to *return* to awareness again and again, each time a little more gently.

I wrote this not as an expert, but as a fellow traveler—someone who has been overwhelmed, distracted, confused, and curious, just like you. Along the way, I discovered that mindfulness is not about changing who you are, but about *noticing* who you already are beneath all the noise.

If even one idea from these pages helps you slow down, breathe deeper, or smile at something you used to overlook, then this book has done its work.

So, take what resonates. Leave what doesn't. But promise yourself this: that you will try to live *deliberately*—not perfectly, not rigidly, but sincerely.

And when life gets loud again (as it always does), may you remember that peace isn't found somewhere far away—it's found right where you are, waiting for you to notice.

Start Where You Are

In the end, the results of practicing mindfulness depend not on me—or any teacher—but entirely on you.

Because mindful living is deeply personal. It's not a rigid path, not a checklist, and certainly not a race.

Let's be honest—it *is* tough. We live in a world of constant motion, surrounded by pings, opinions, deadlines, and desires. We juggle work, relationships, bills, and endless digital noise. There will always be a hundred reasons not to begin: "I'm too busy." "I live in a noisy place." "My job doesn't allow it." "Maybe later." But sometimes, all it takes is one strong reason to begin—the quiet desire to improve your own state of mind, well-being, and inner peace.

Harmony between humans and nature is still possible. We don't need to fight the world to find peace in it. The idea isn't to escape modern life or reject progress—it's to balance the primitive and the modern, to find simplicity within complexity. That harmony begins when we stop waging a war with nature and instead learn to live *with* it.

Start by caring, genuinely caring—for your surroundings, for your body, for your neighbors, for the next generation. We cannot keep complaining about systems while ignoring the small actions we can take every day as mindful, educated citizens. You don't have to overhaul your entire life to live consciously. Just declutter one shelf, take one mindful walk, pause for one deep breath before reacting, or resist one unnecessary purchase. Small acts done consistently lead to lasting change.

Because the truth is, there is no finish line in mindful living. No "perfect" version of peace. It's a practice, a rhythm, a choice you make every single day. And once you begin, you'll notice something beautiful—how your surroundings start to mirror your inner calm, how chaos feels less overwhelming, how joy starts showing up in simple things again.

You don't need a mountain or a monastery to begin. You can start right now, from a quiet corner of your room—with your phone on silent, your mind open, and your heart willing.

Mindful living is not about becoming someone new.

It's about coming home to yourself—slowly, gently, and fully awake.

🙞 Final Reflection

"The art of mindful living begins not with changing the world, but with changing how you see it."

✦ What's one small change you can make today to live more consciously?

✦ Can you promise yourself to start—not perfectly, but sincerely?

With warmth and gratitude,

Phalguni